# MUSE
## MADISON TEASE

©2018 Madison Tease
All rights reserved.

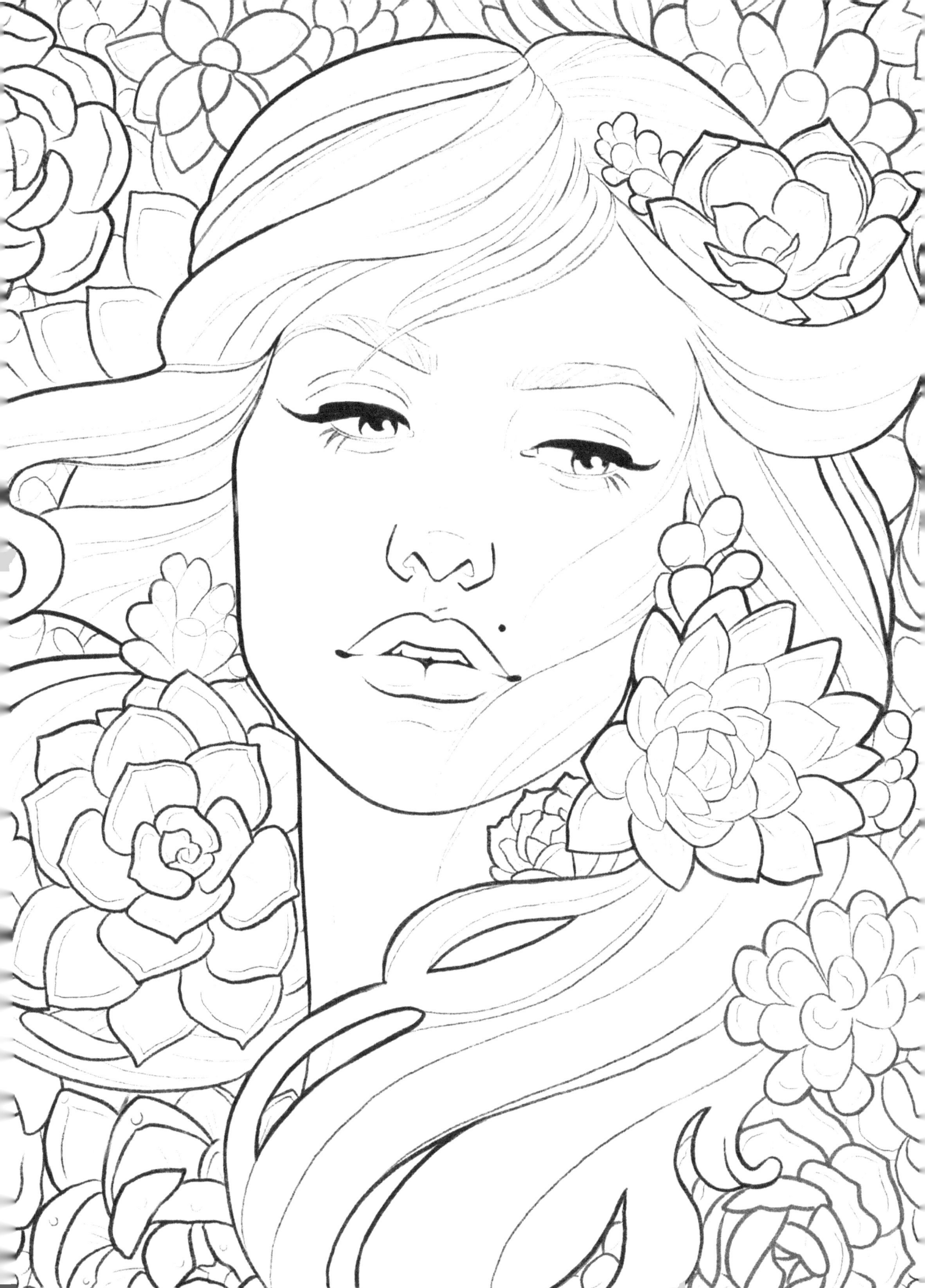

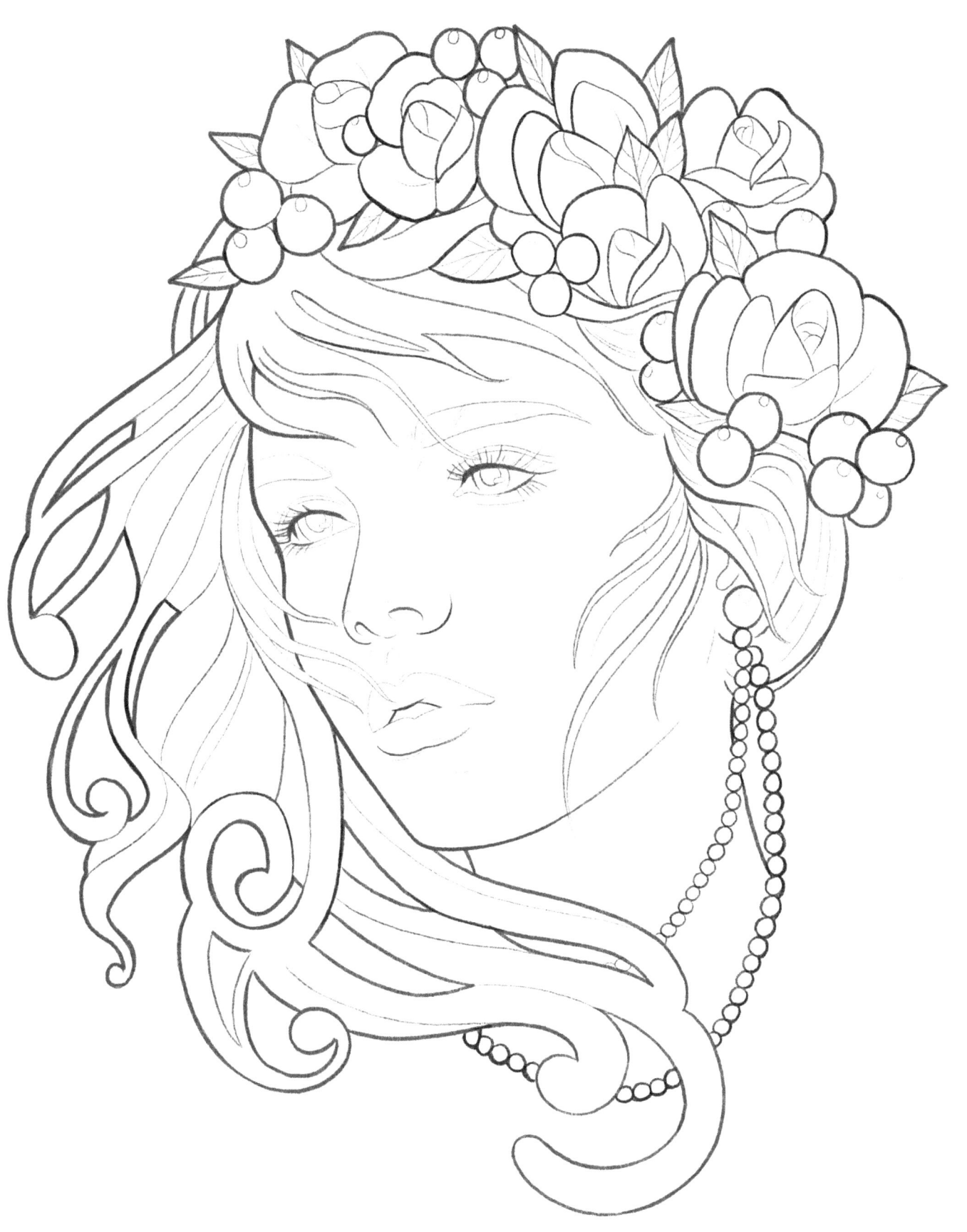

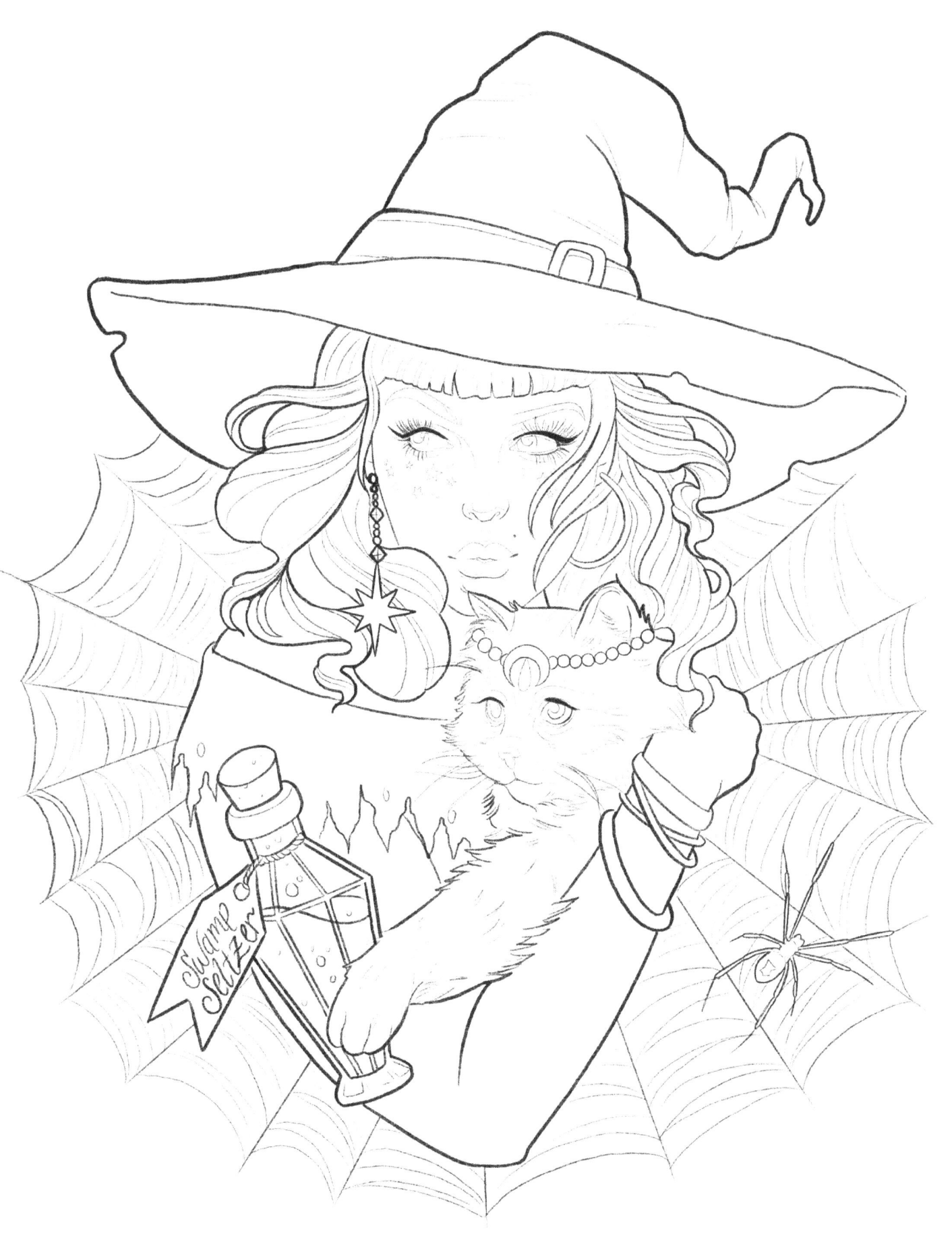

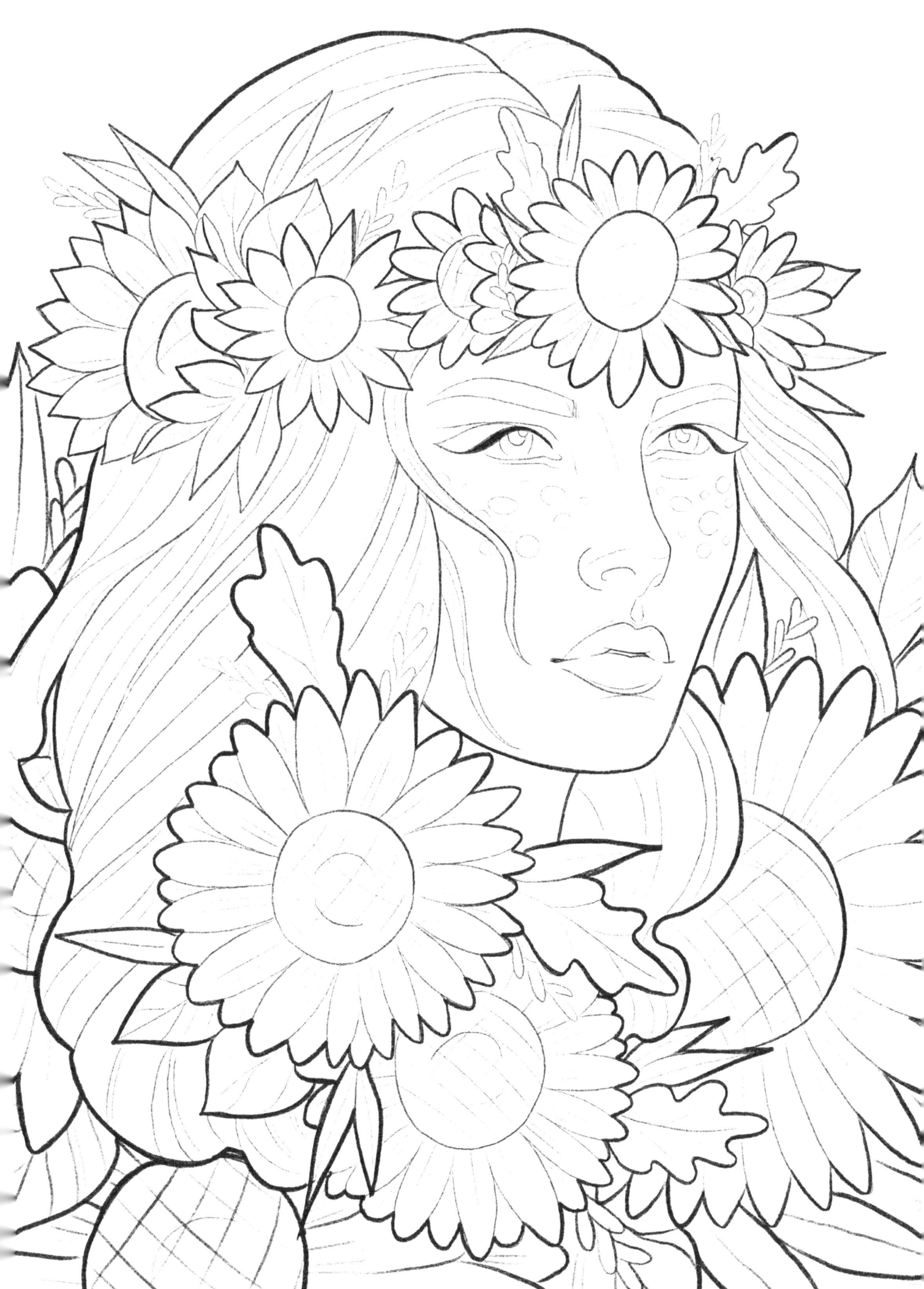

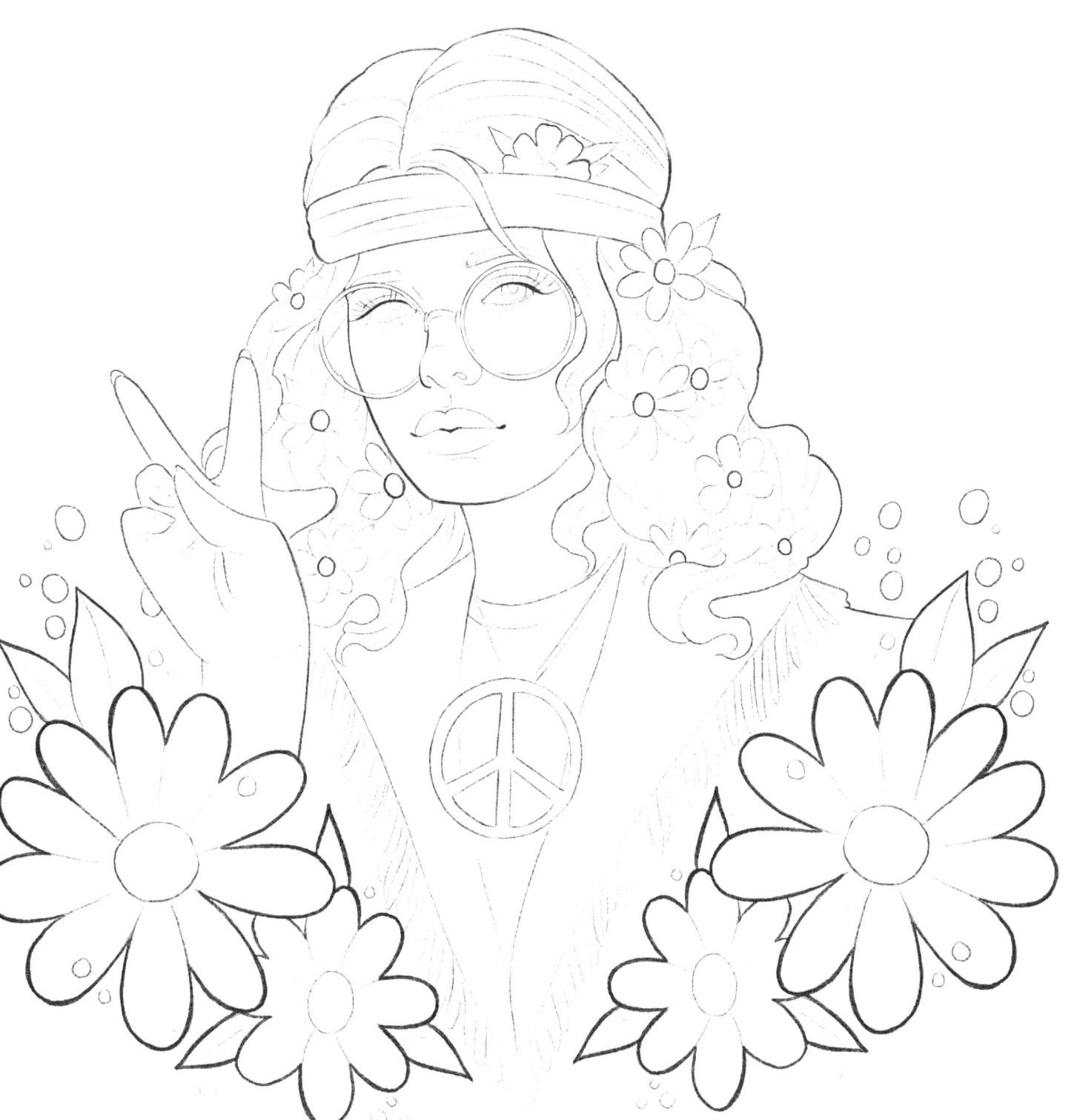

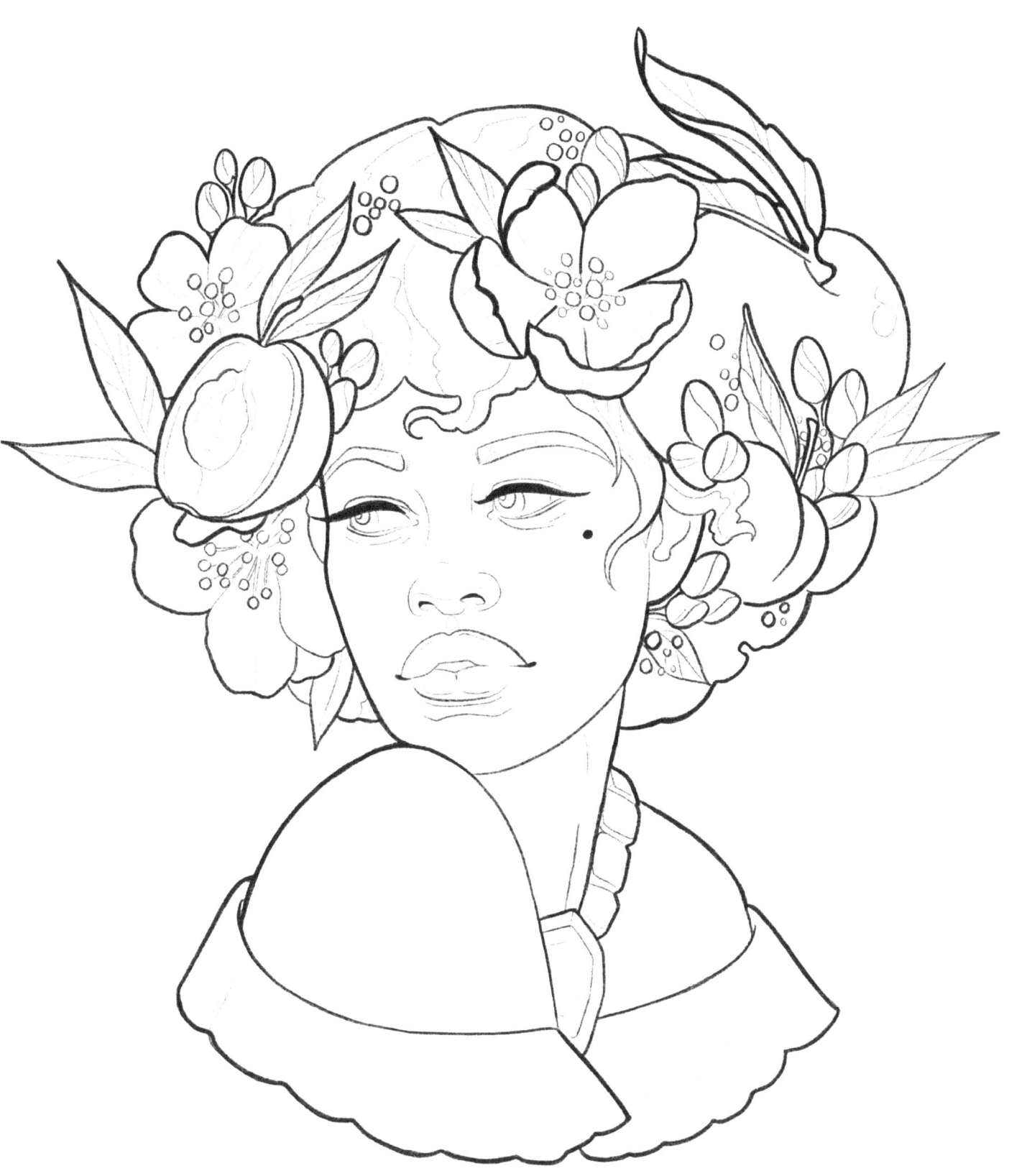

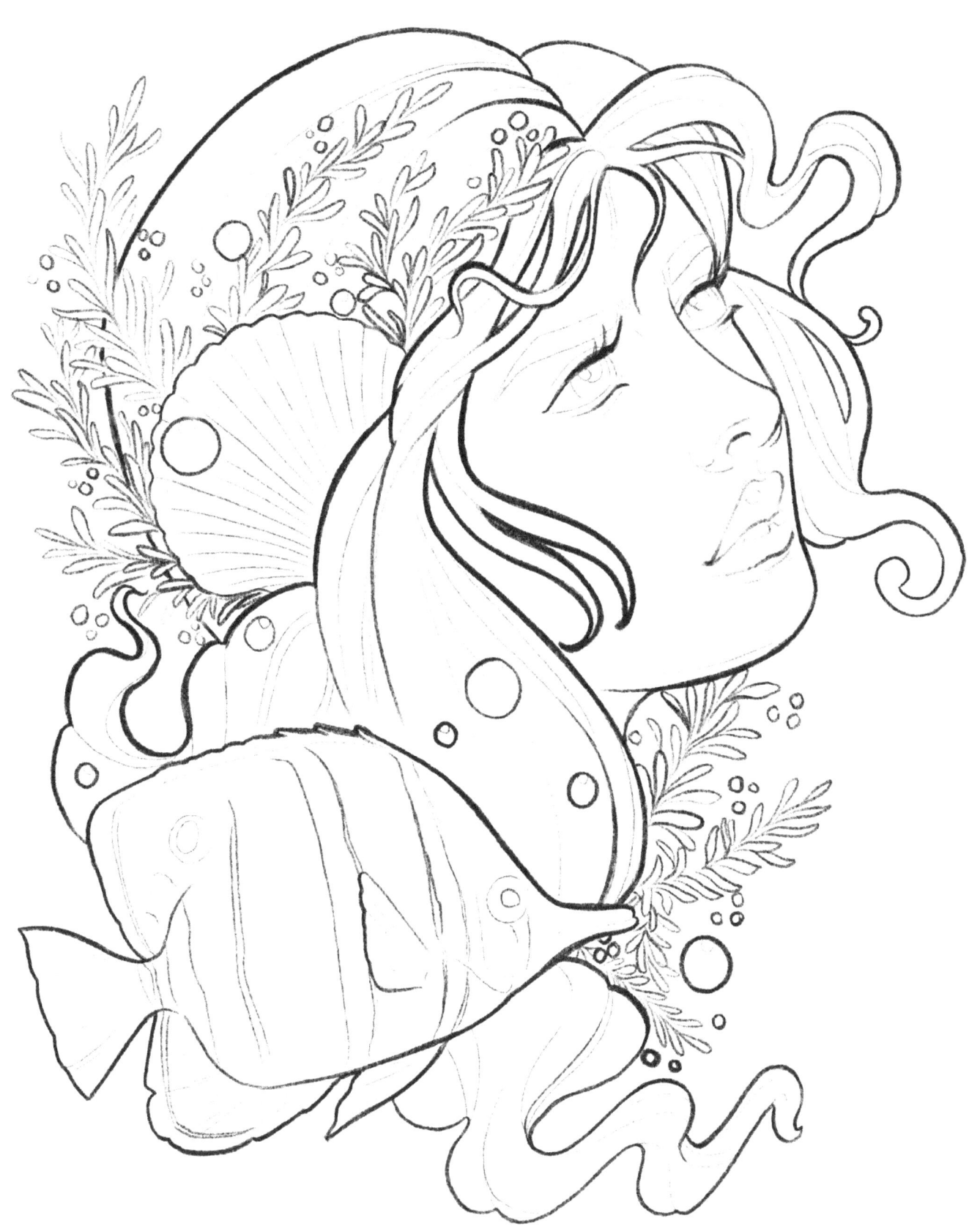

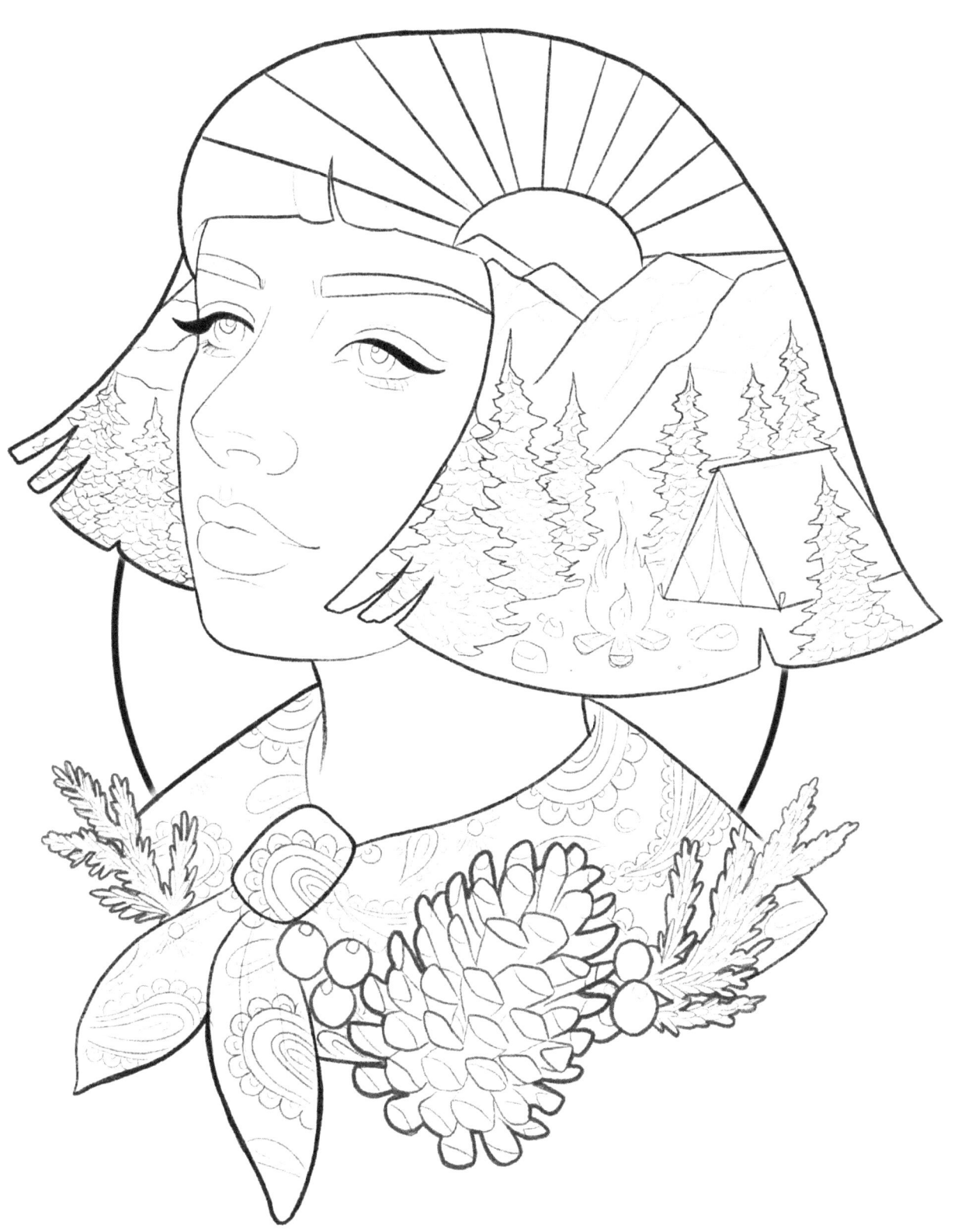

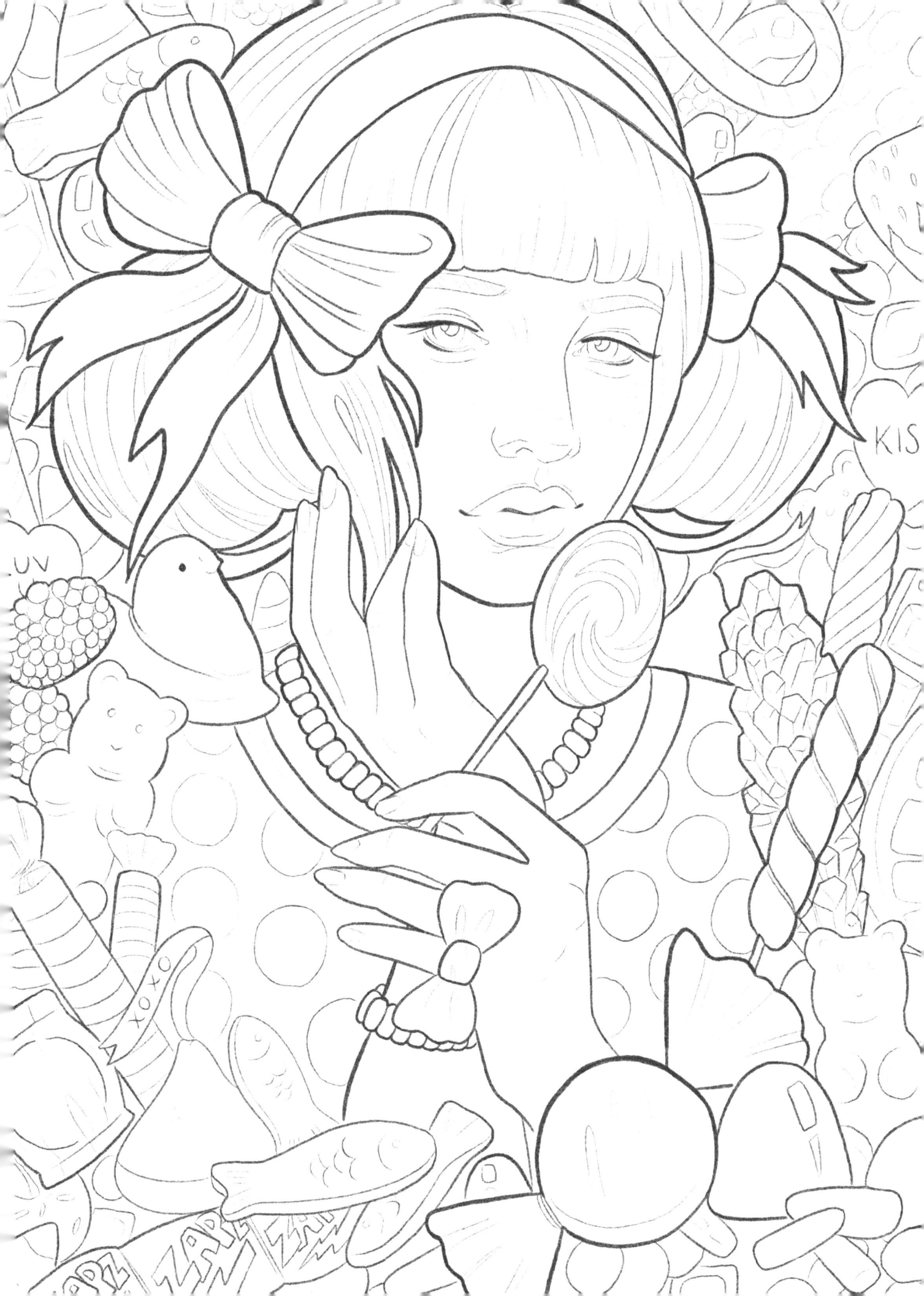

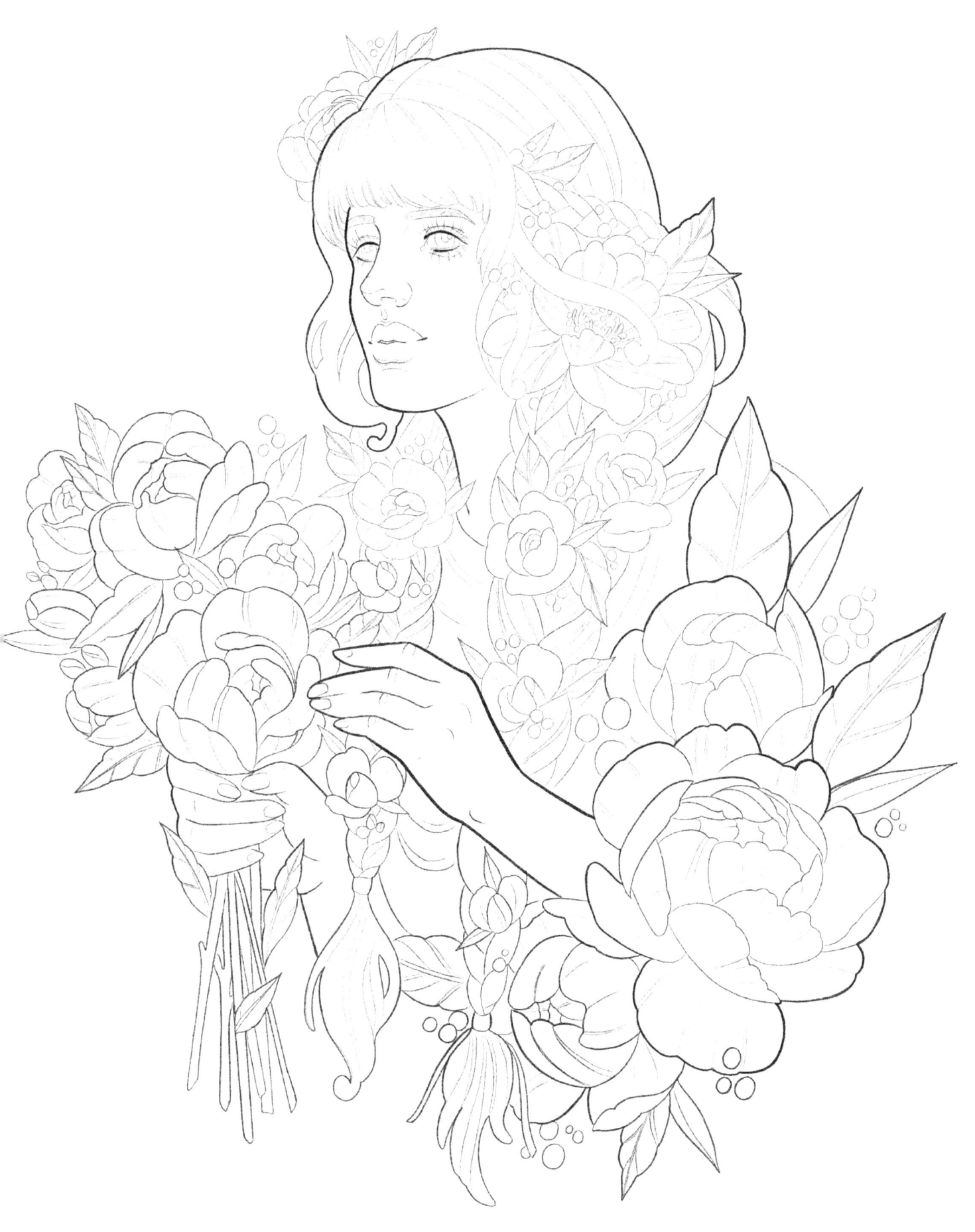

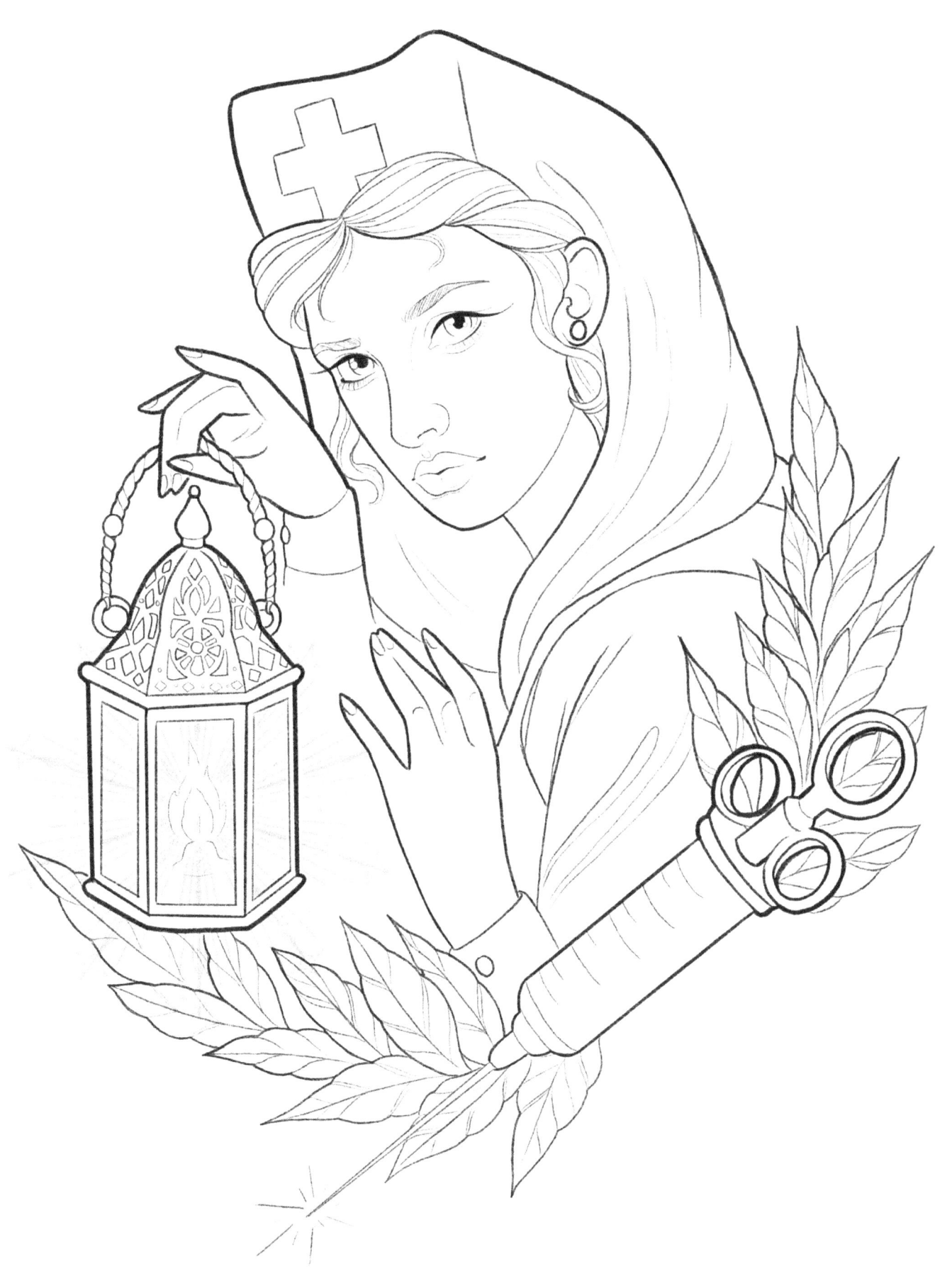

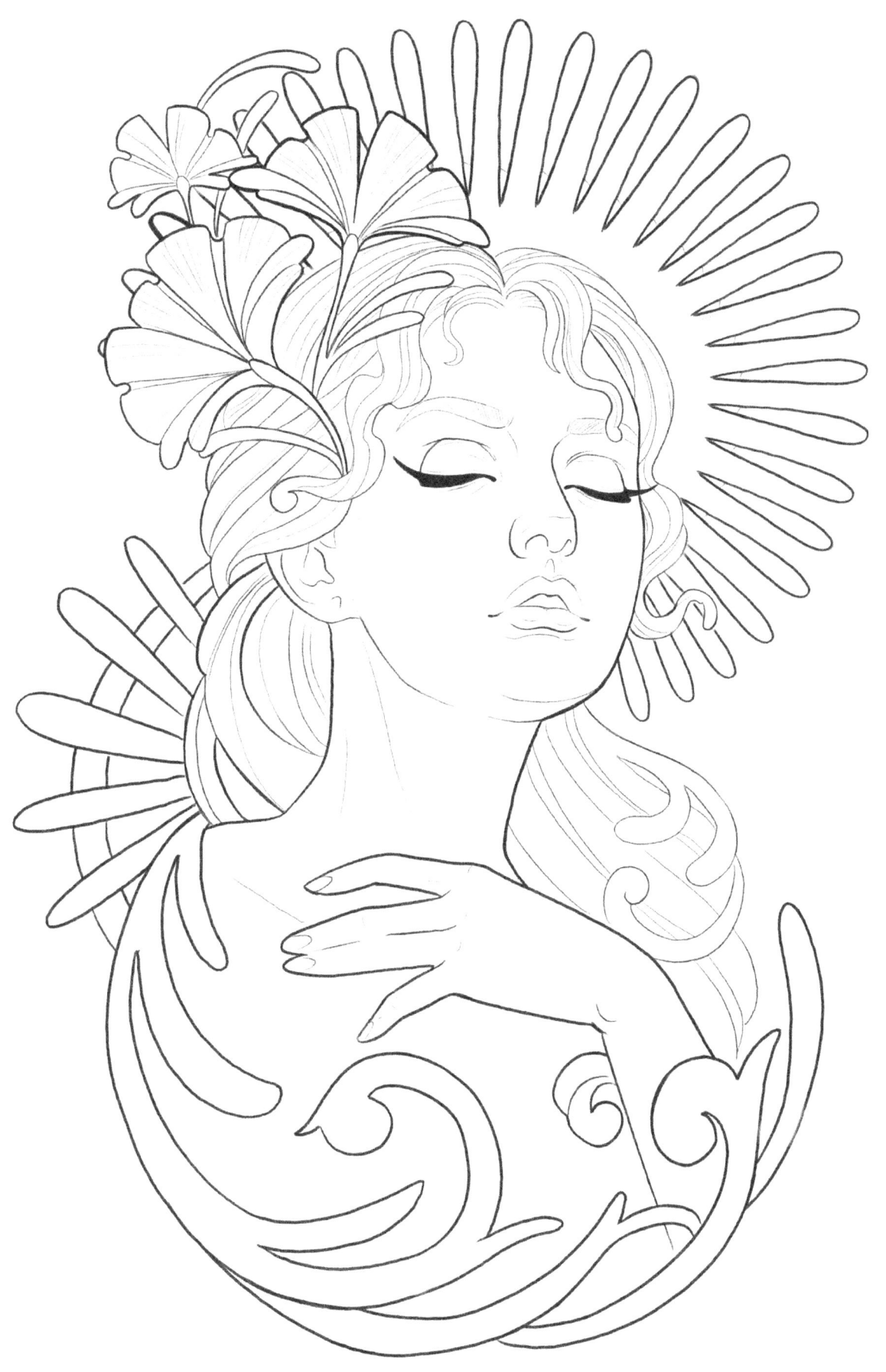

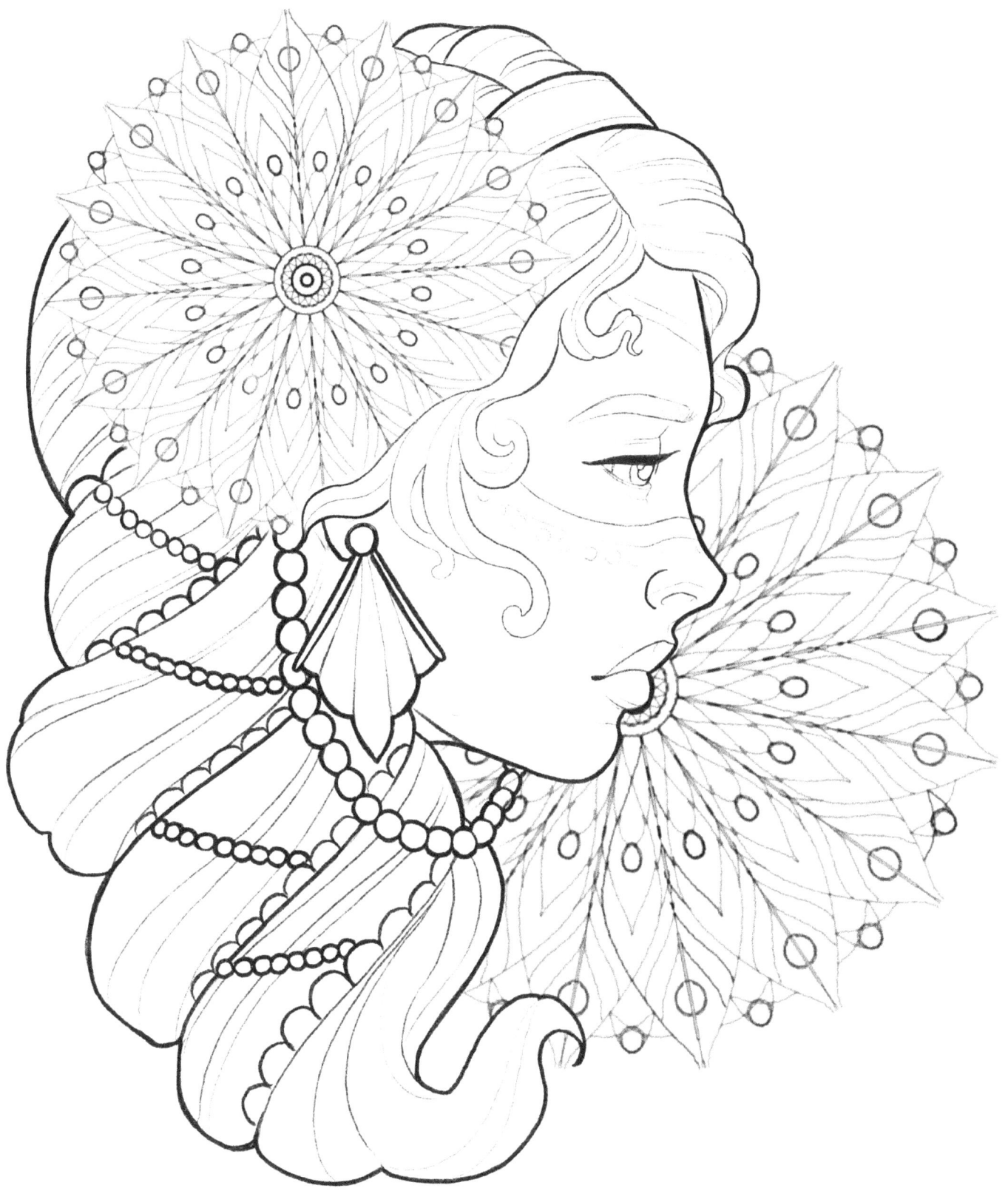

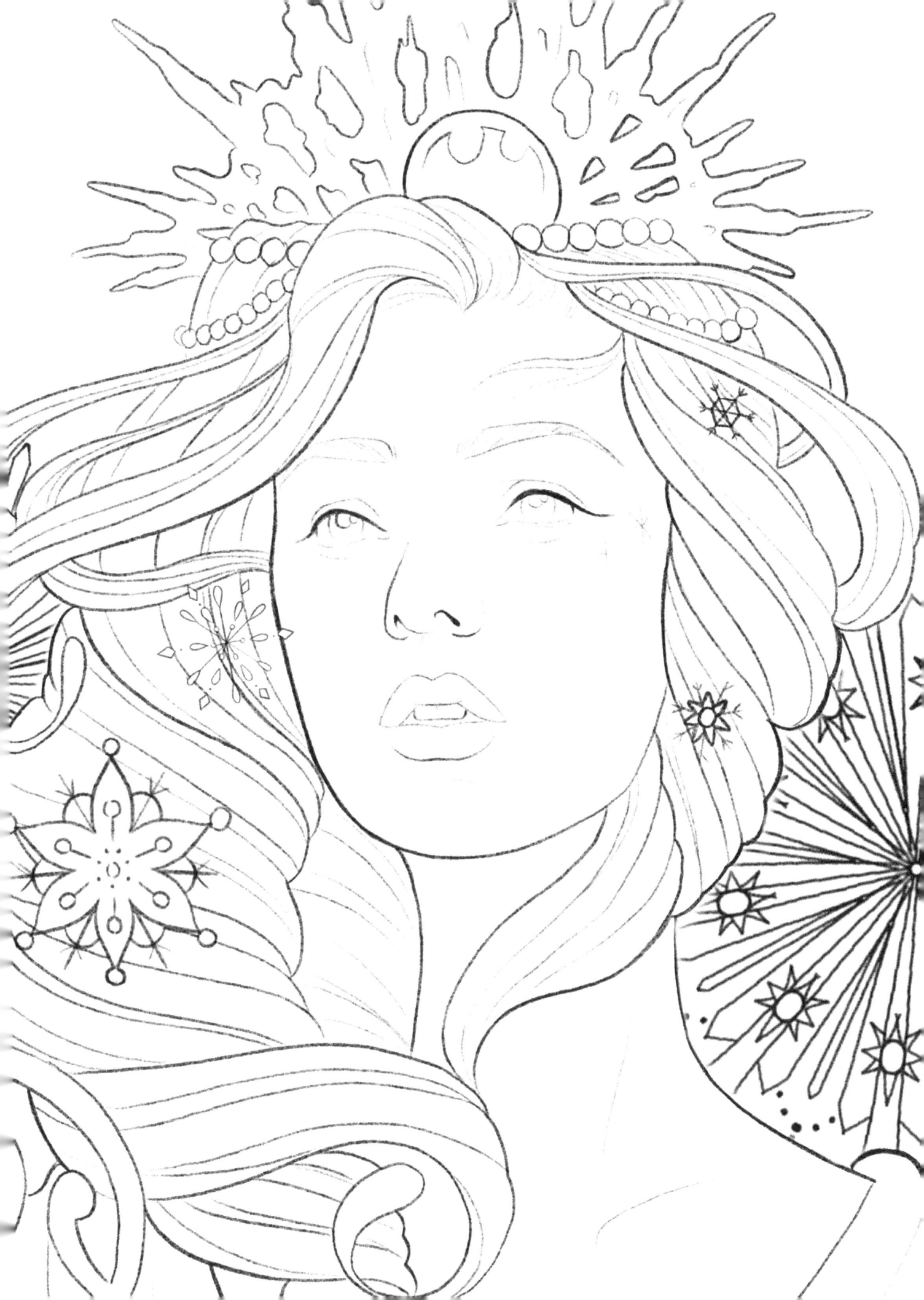

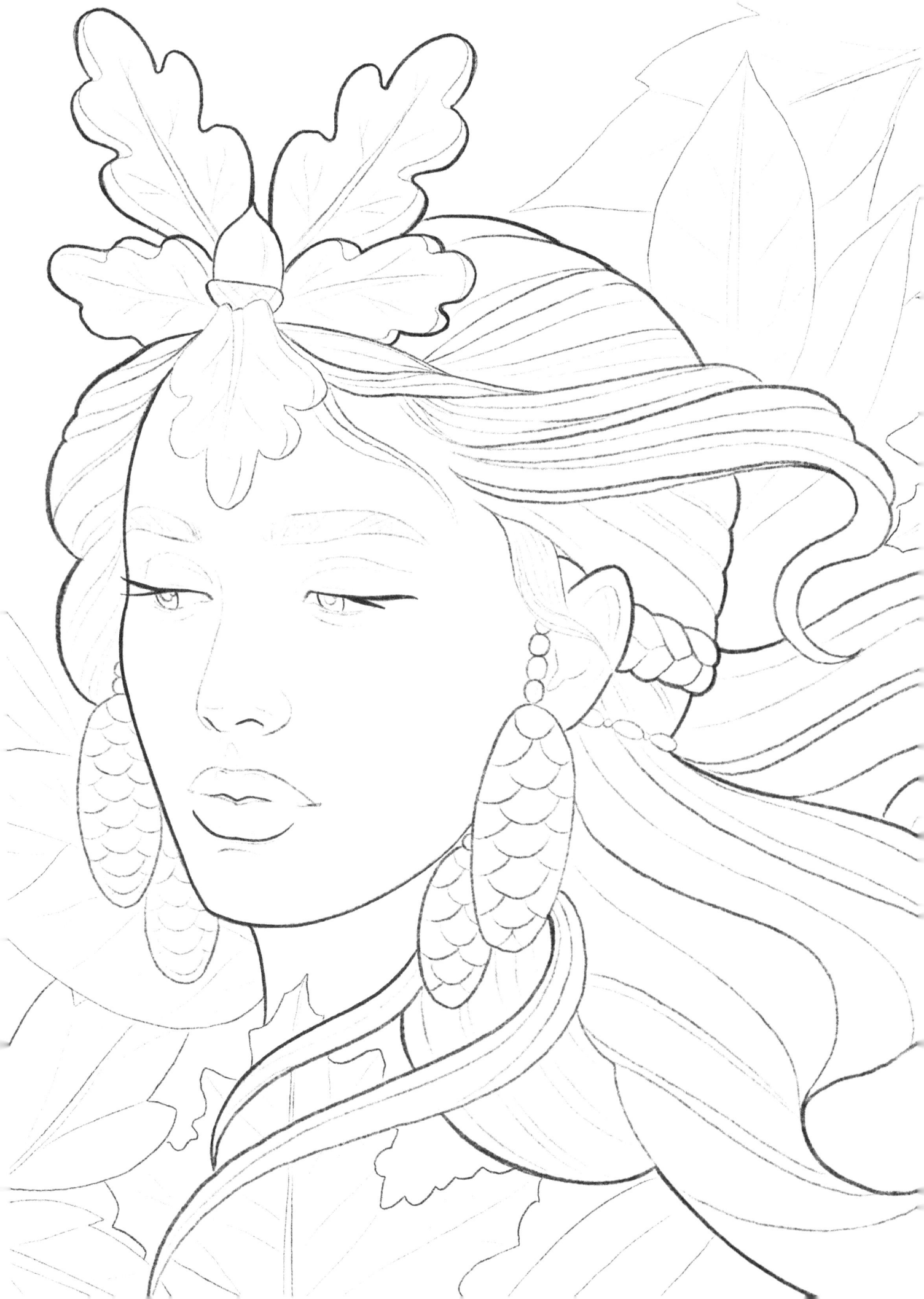

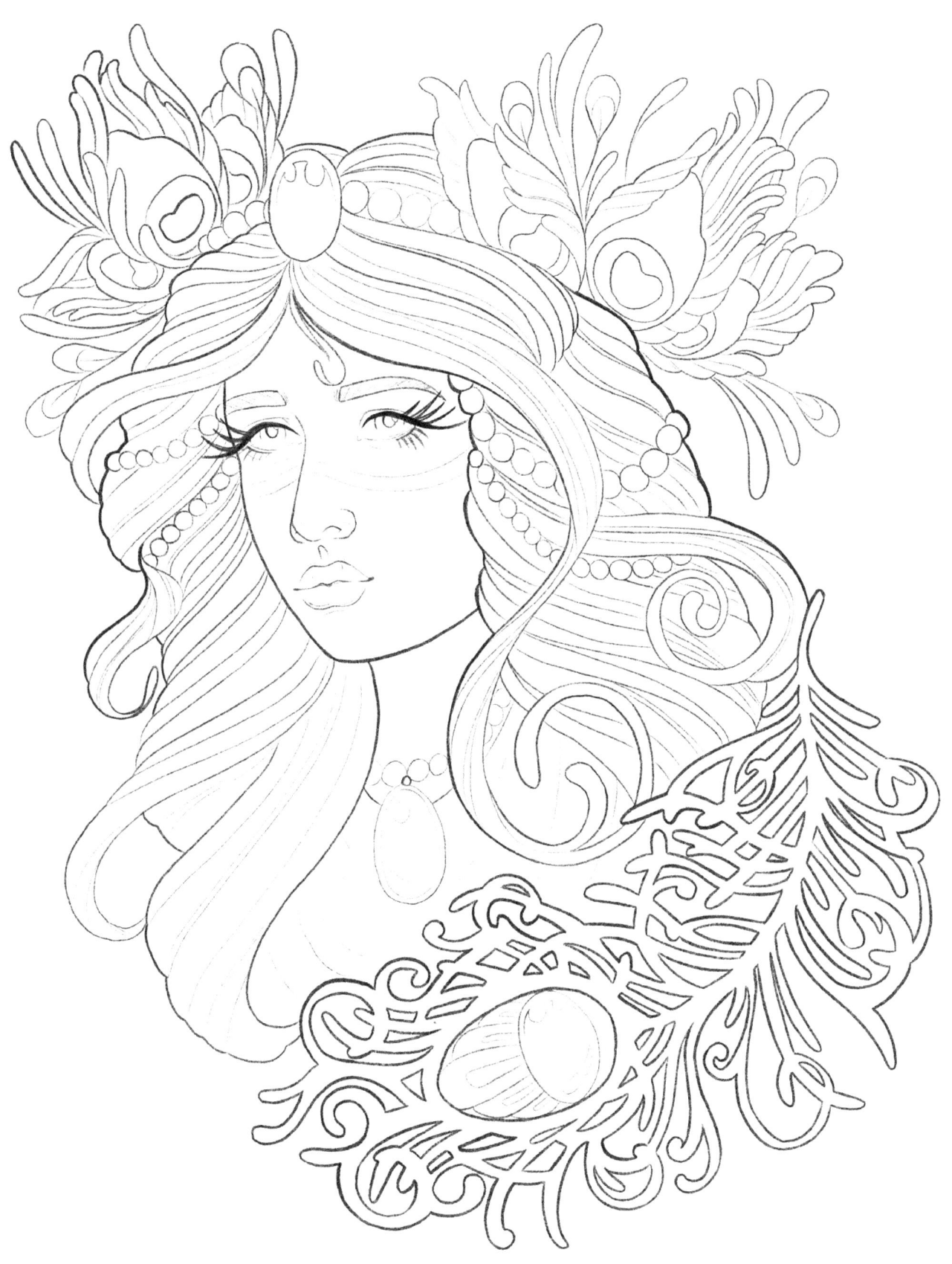

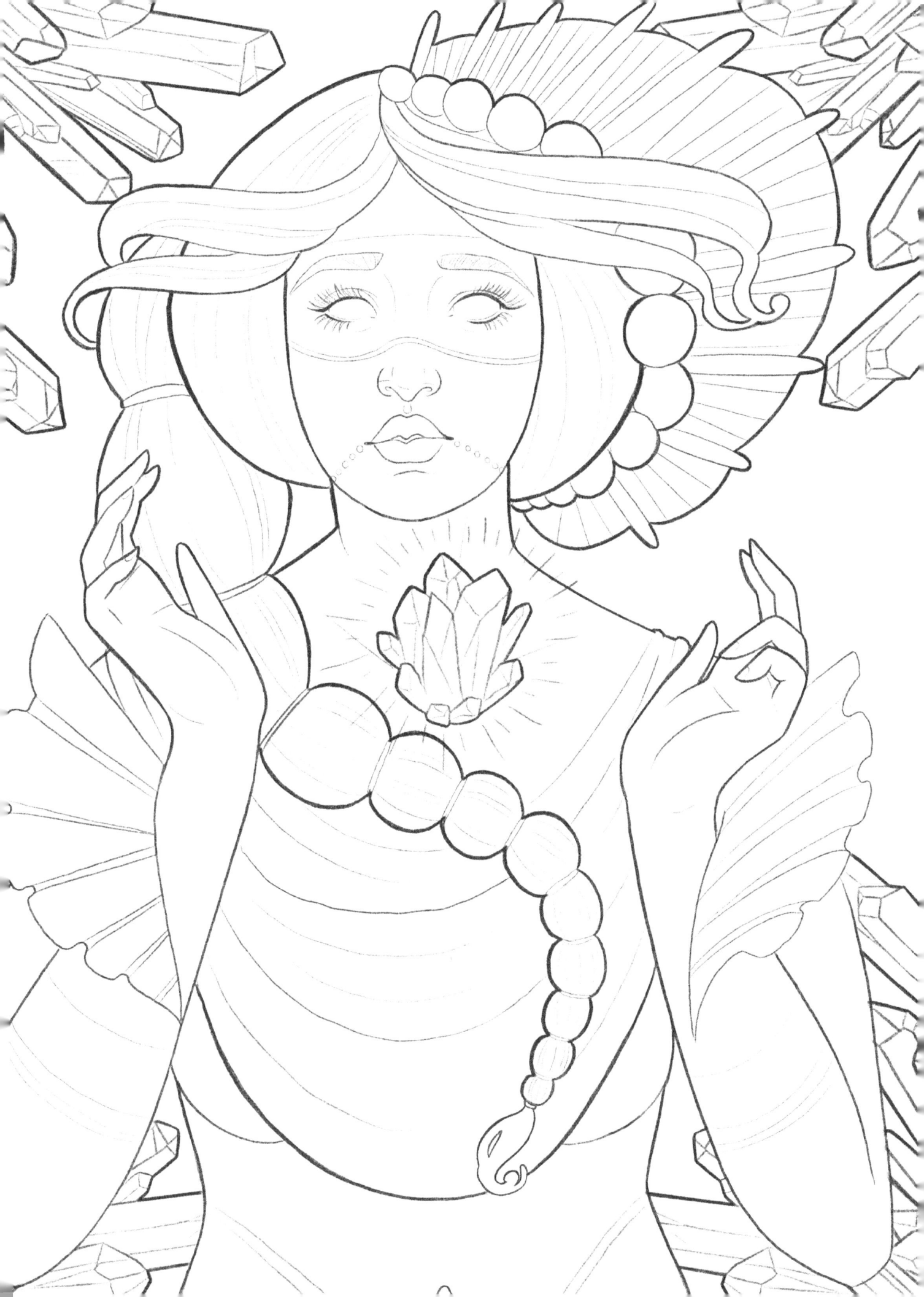

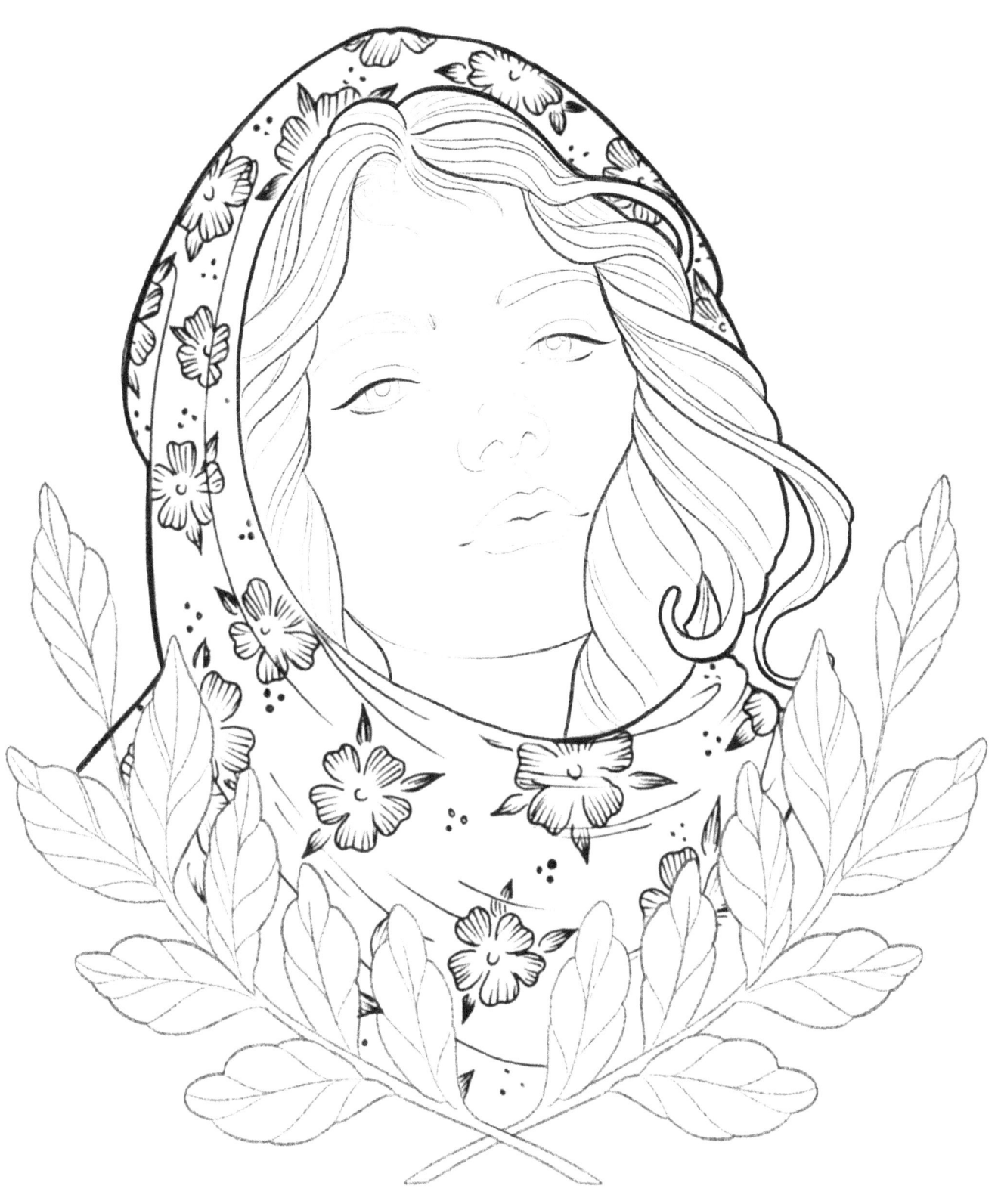

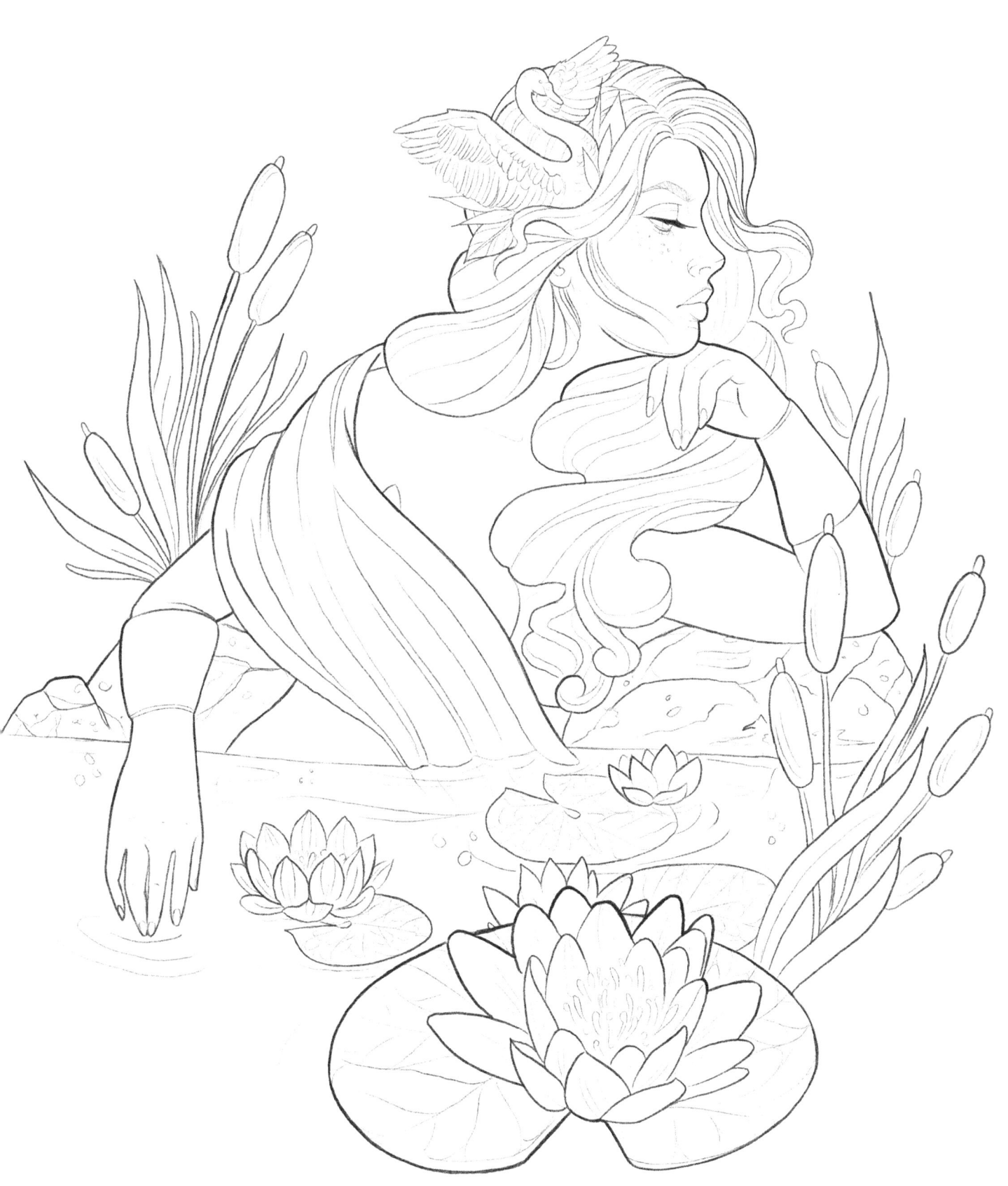

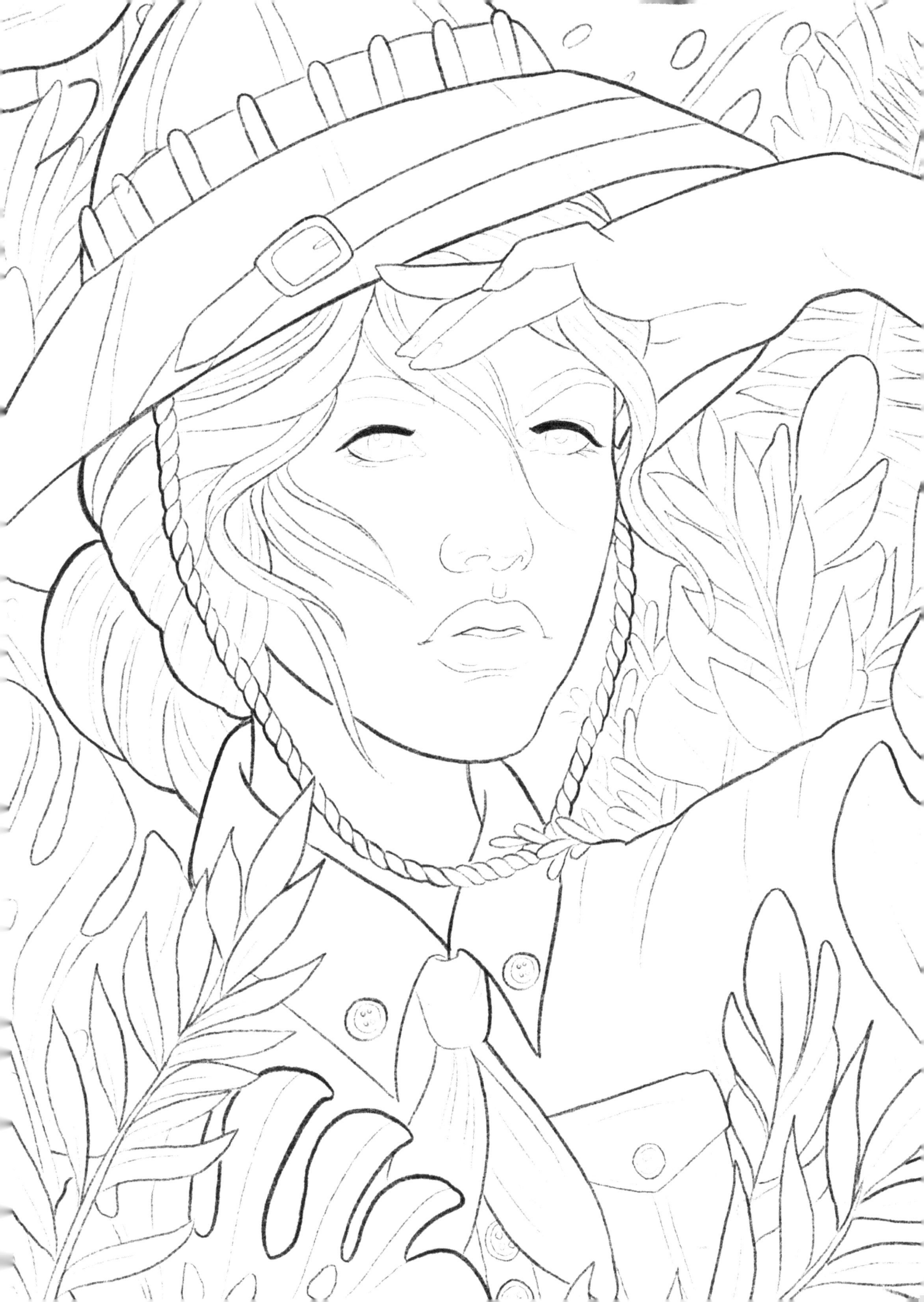

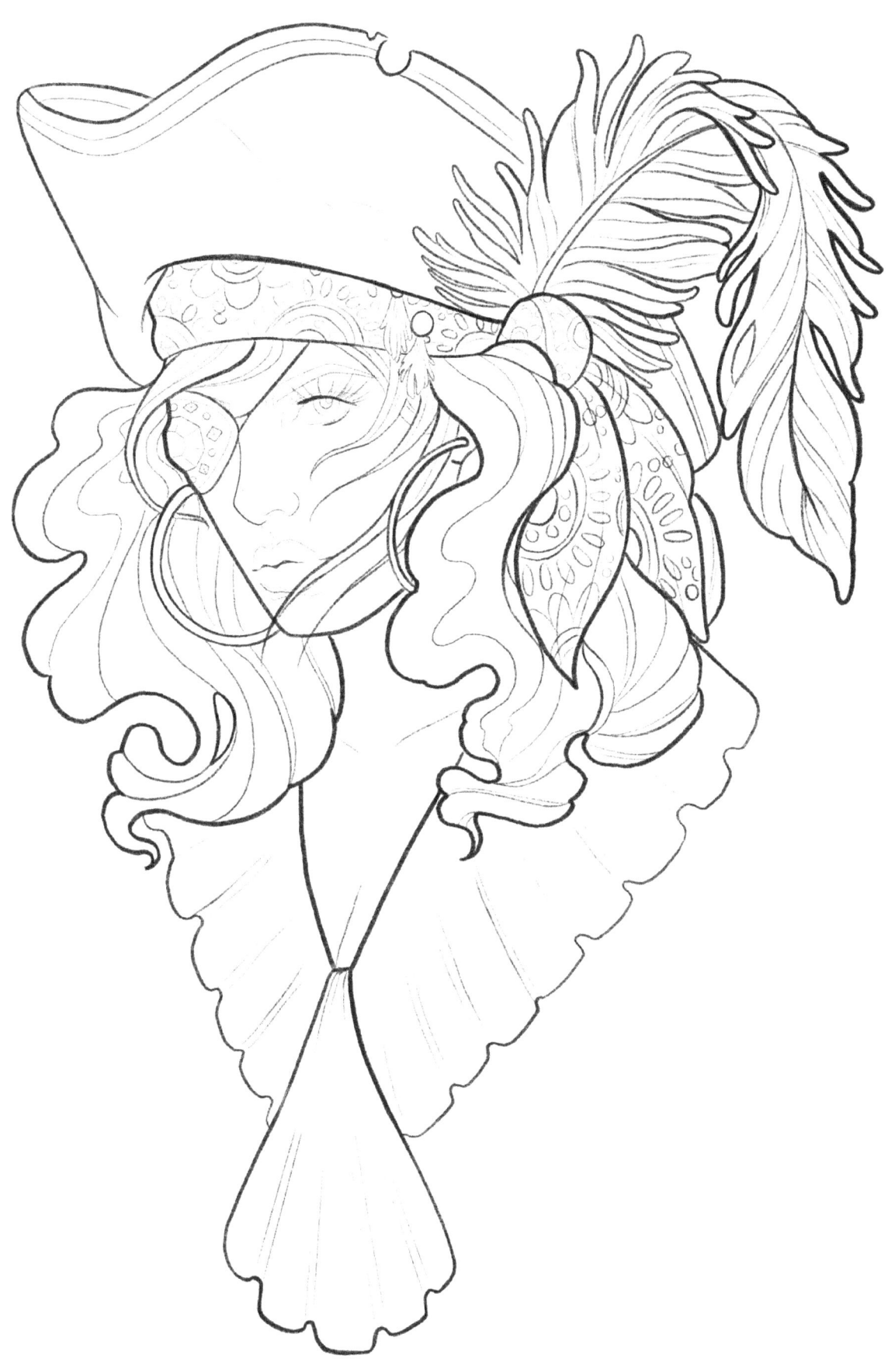

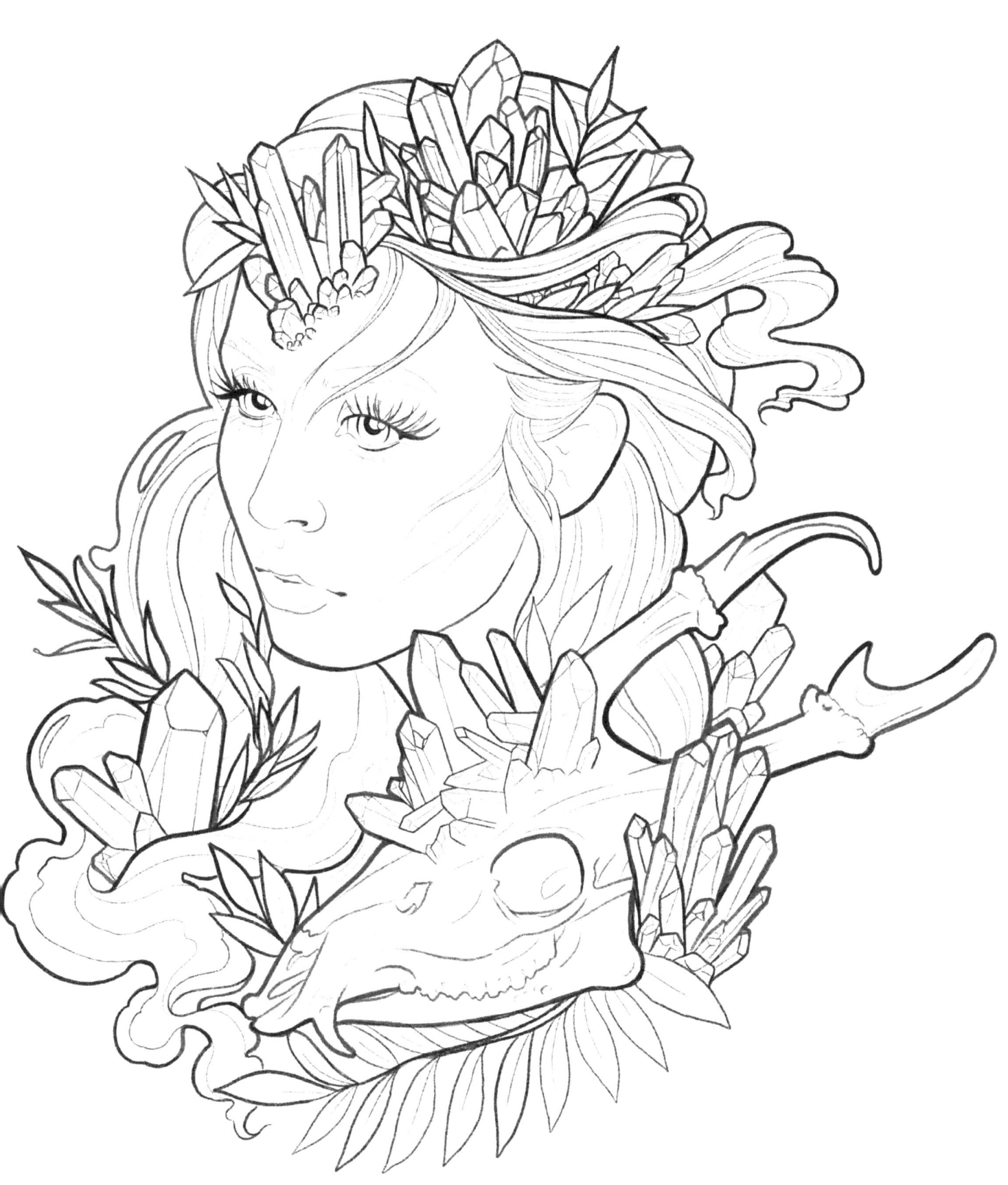

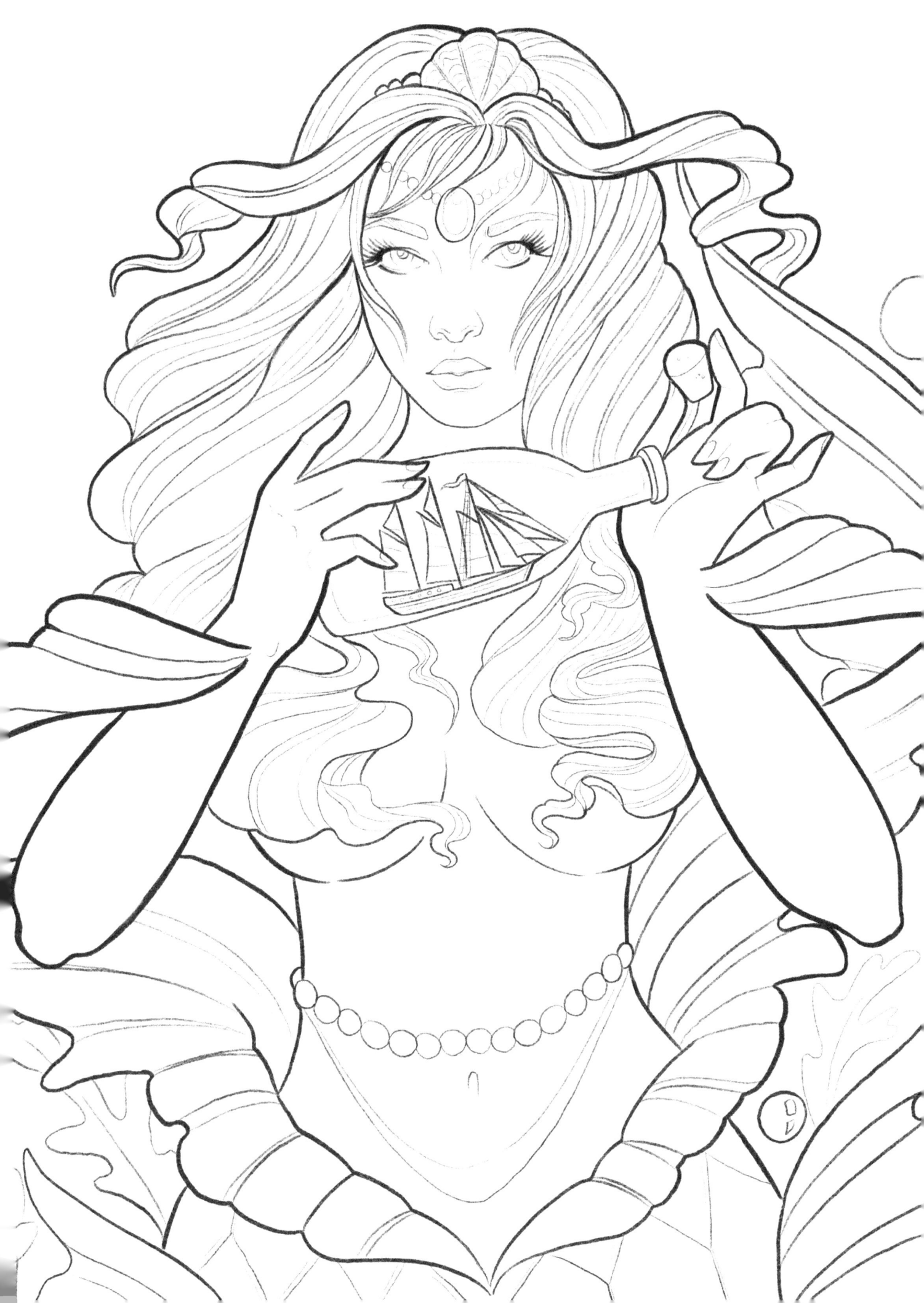

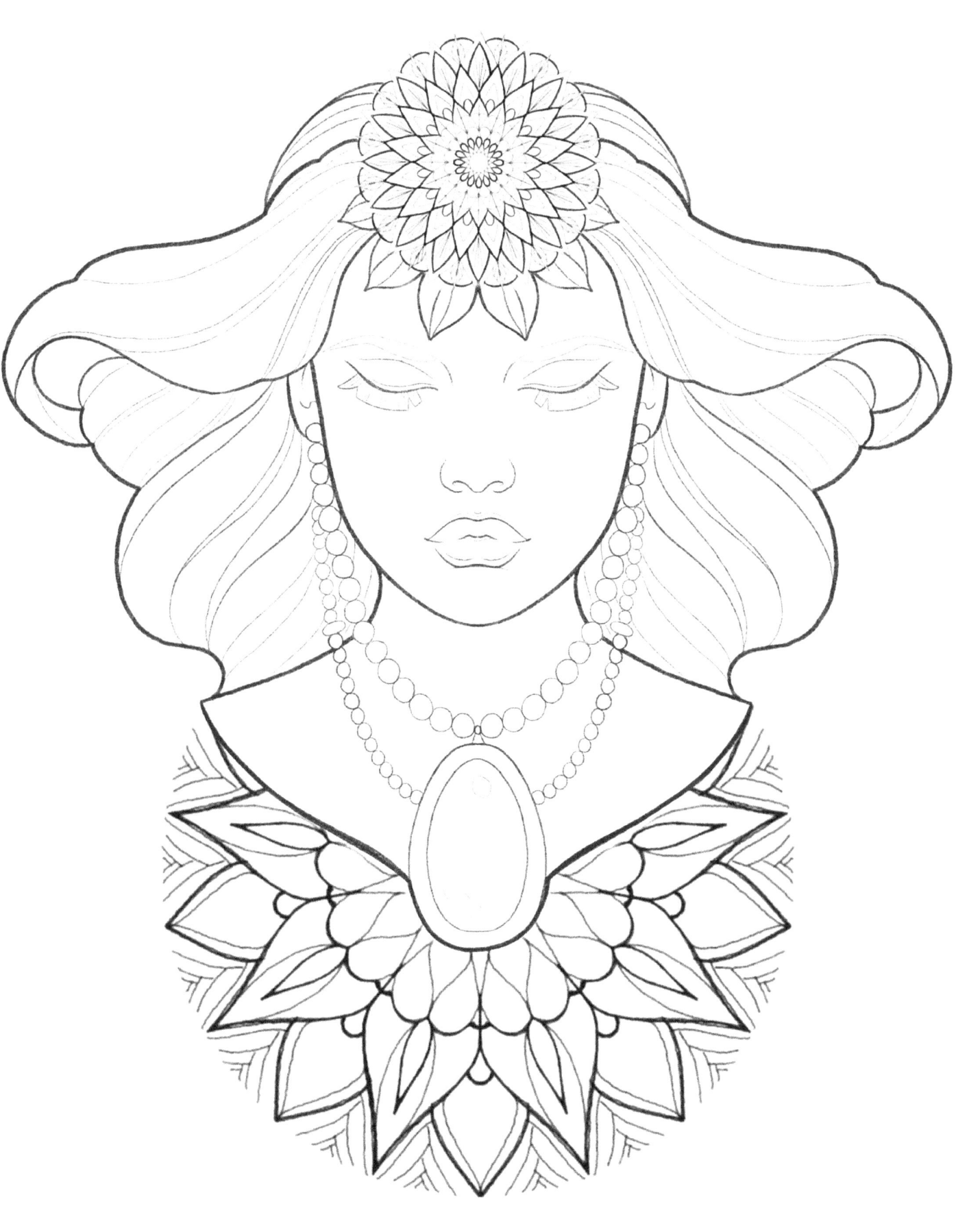

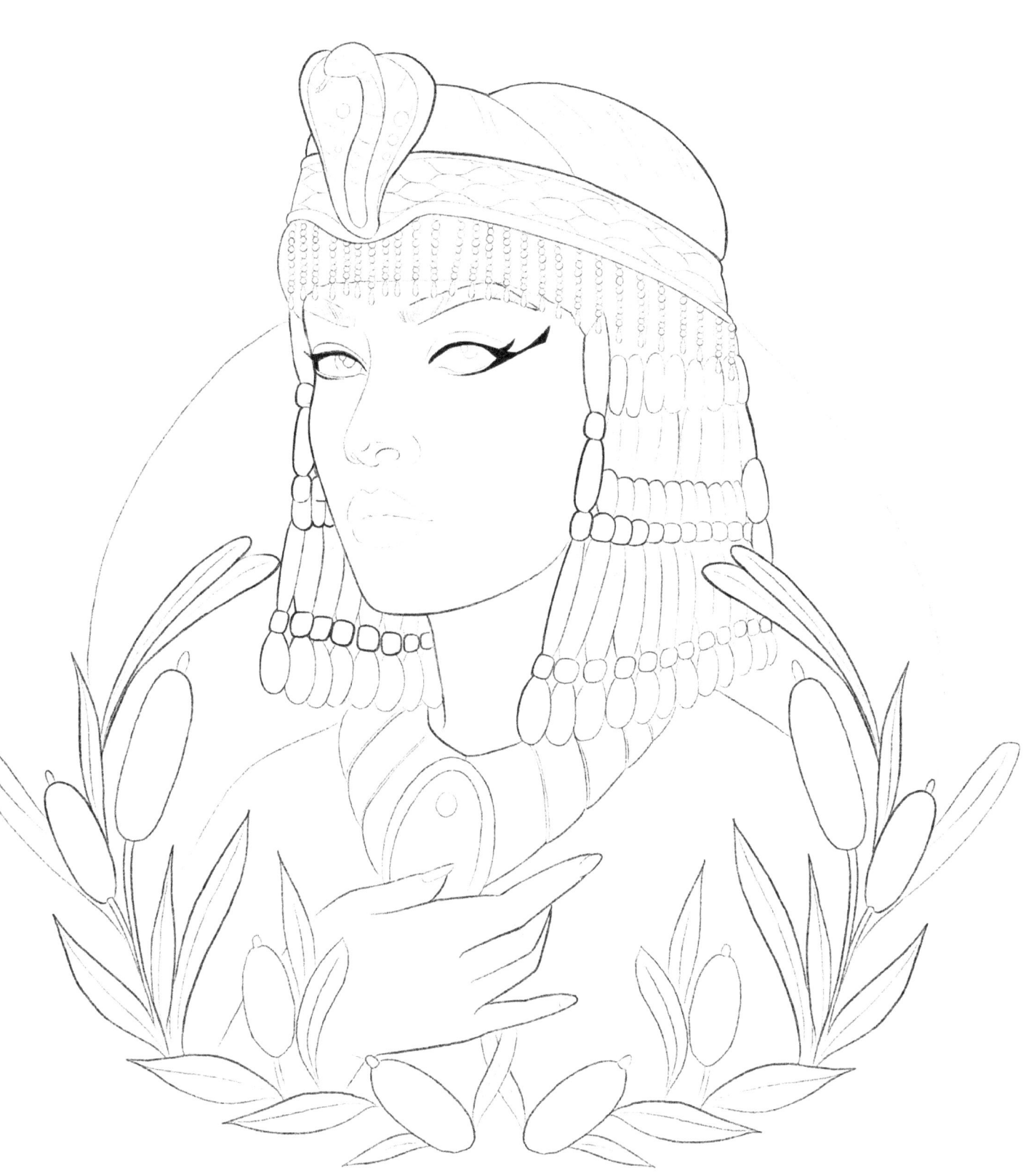

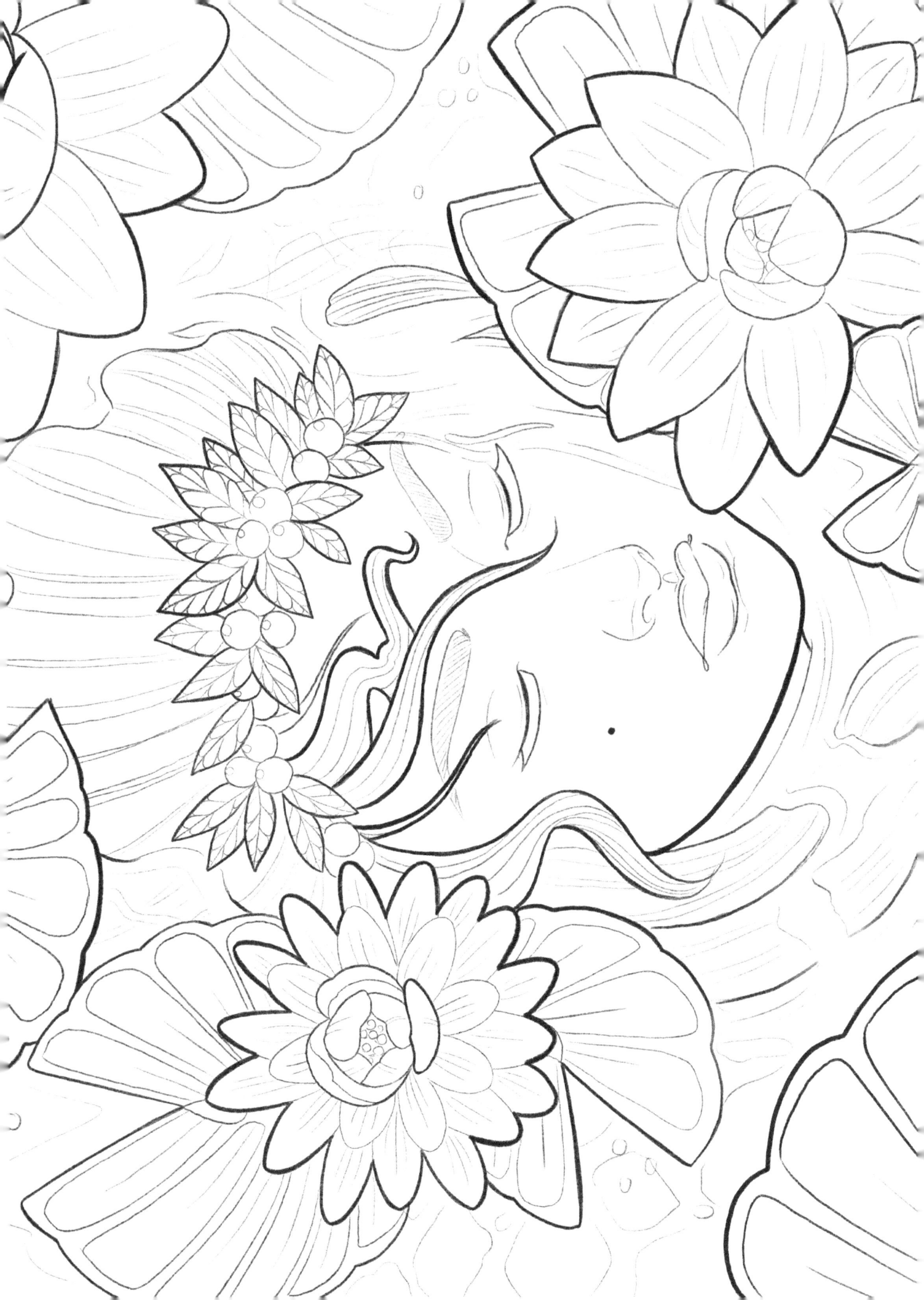

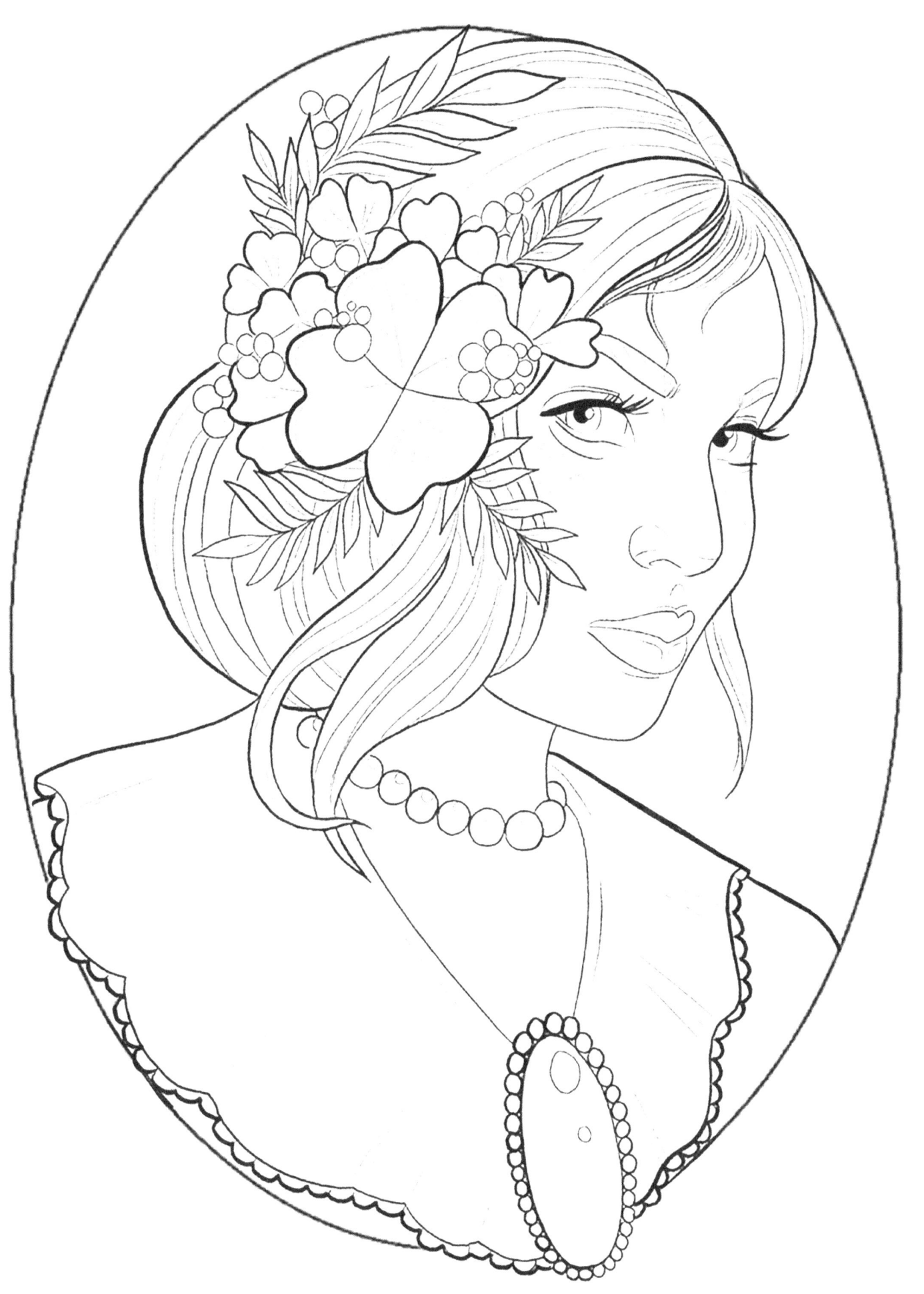

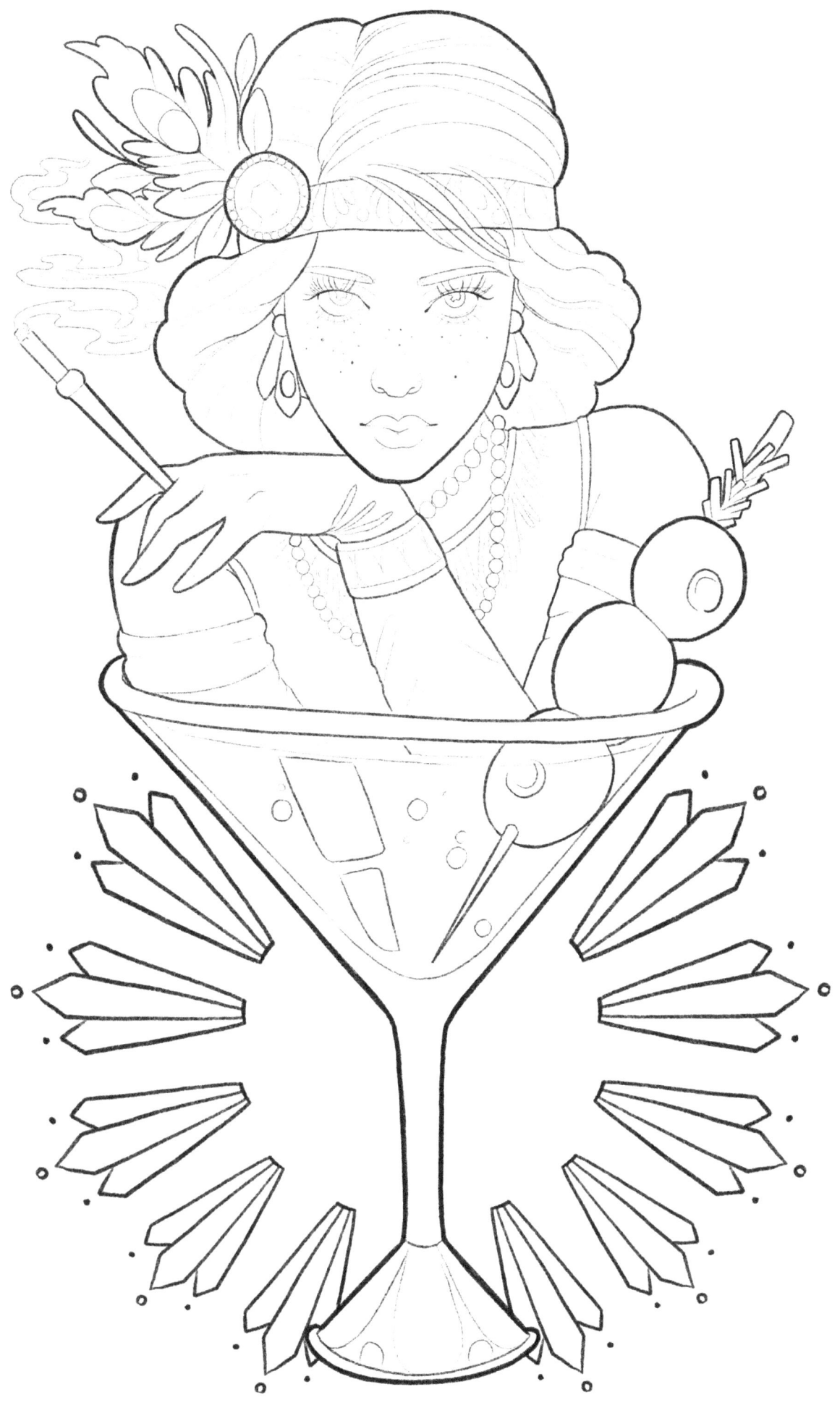

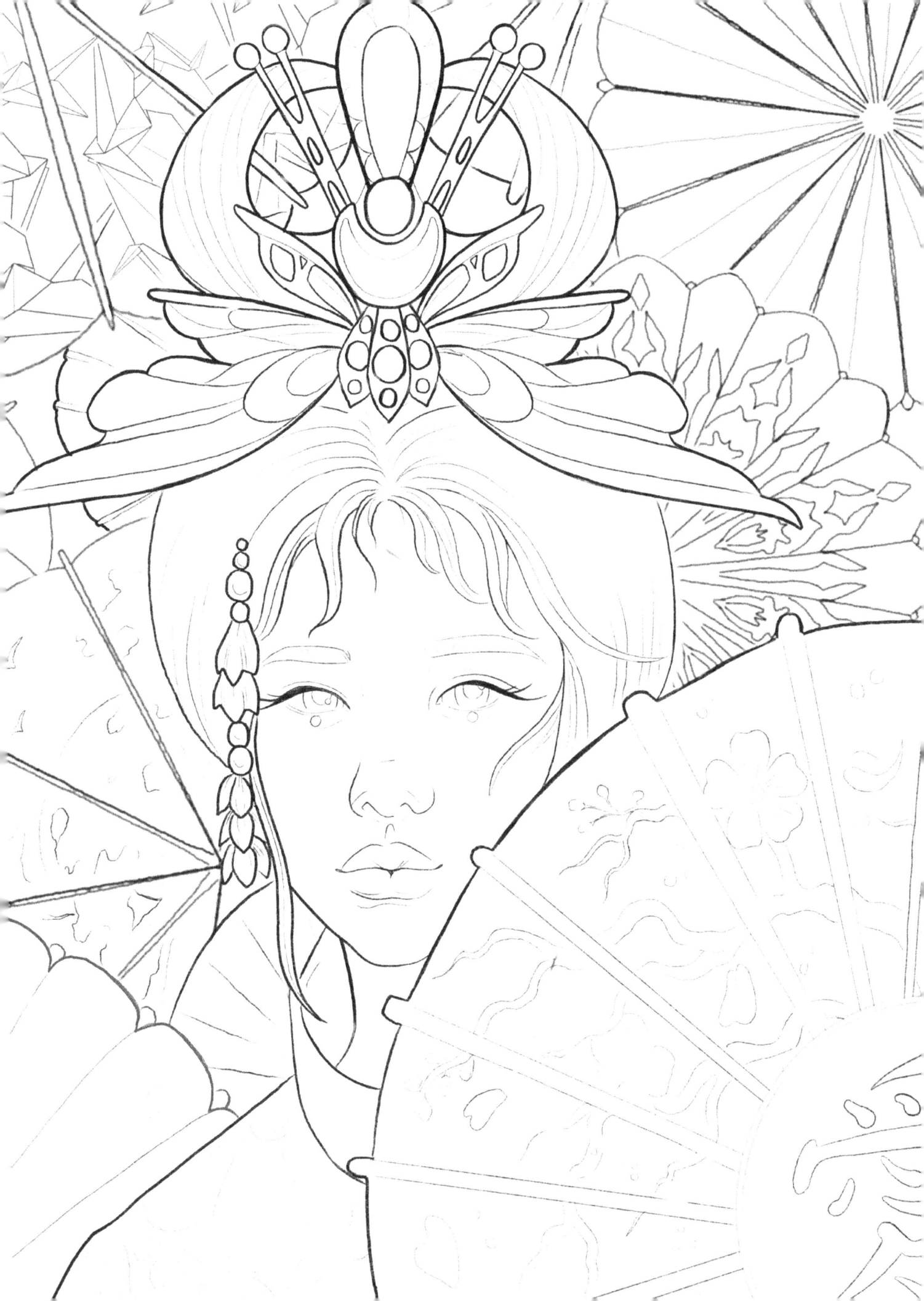

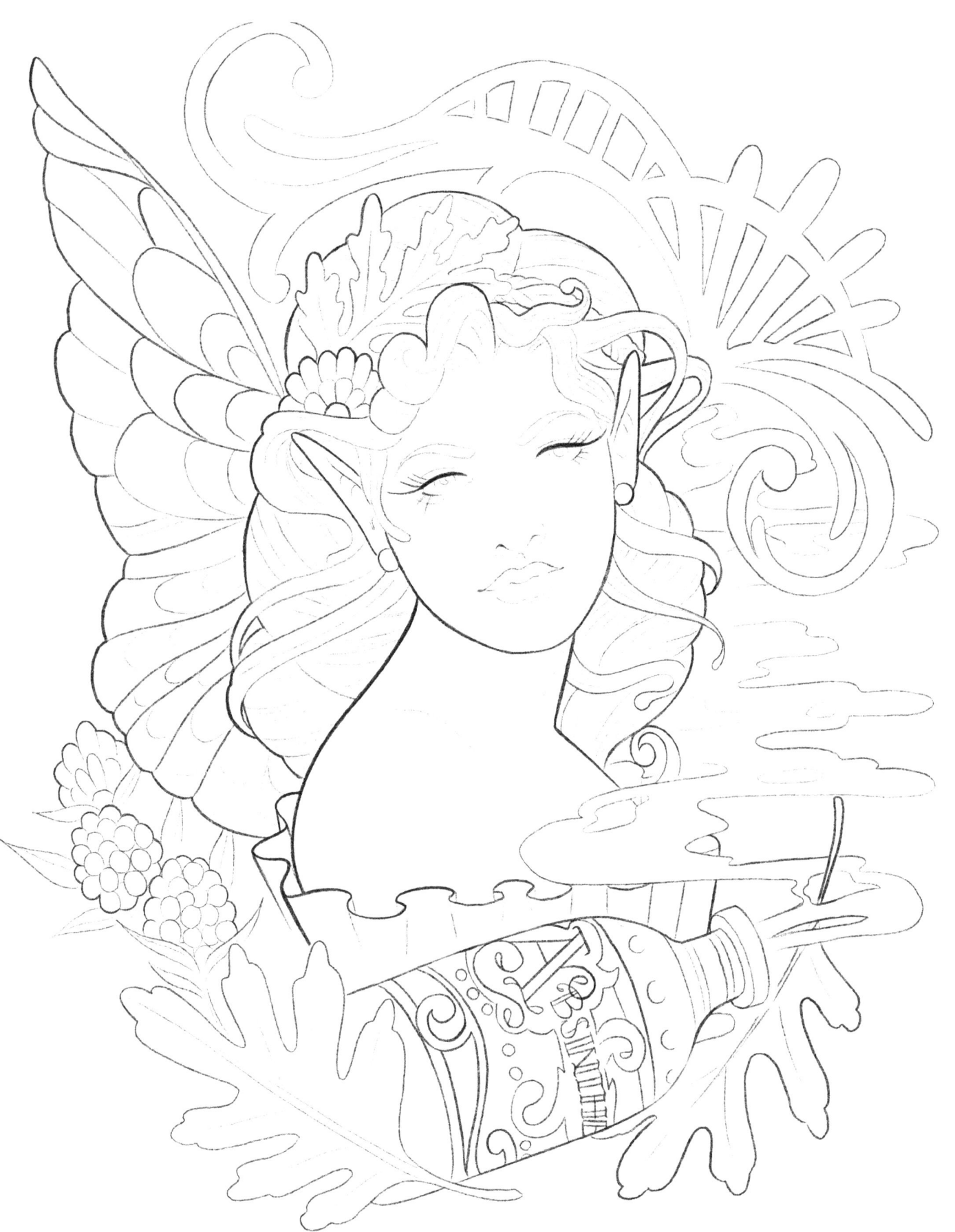

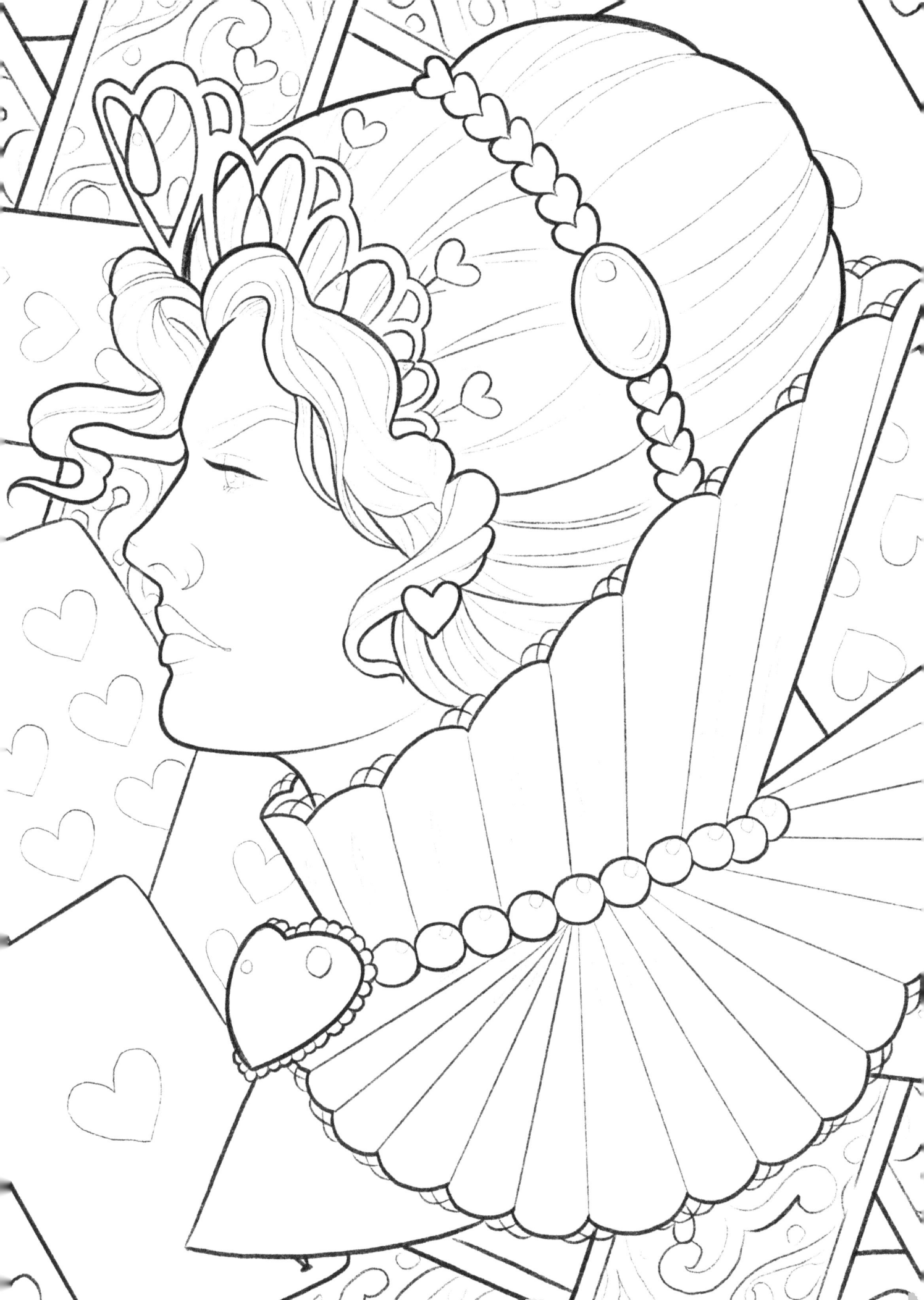

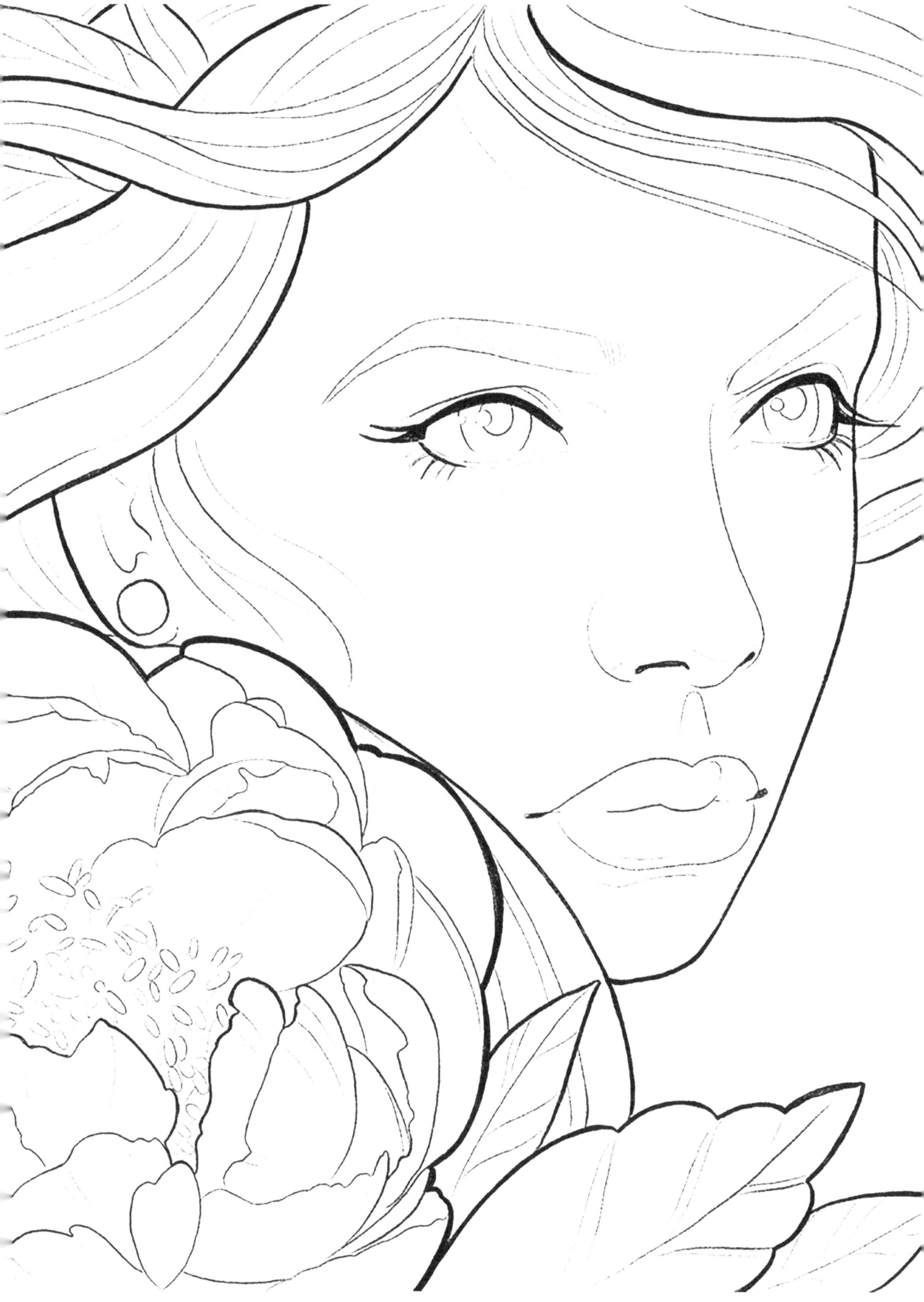

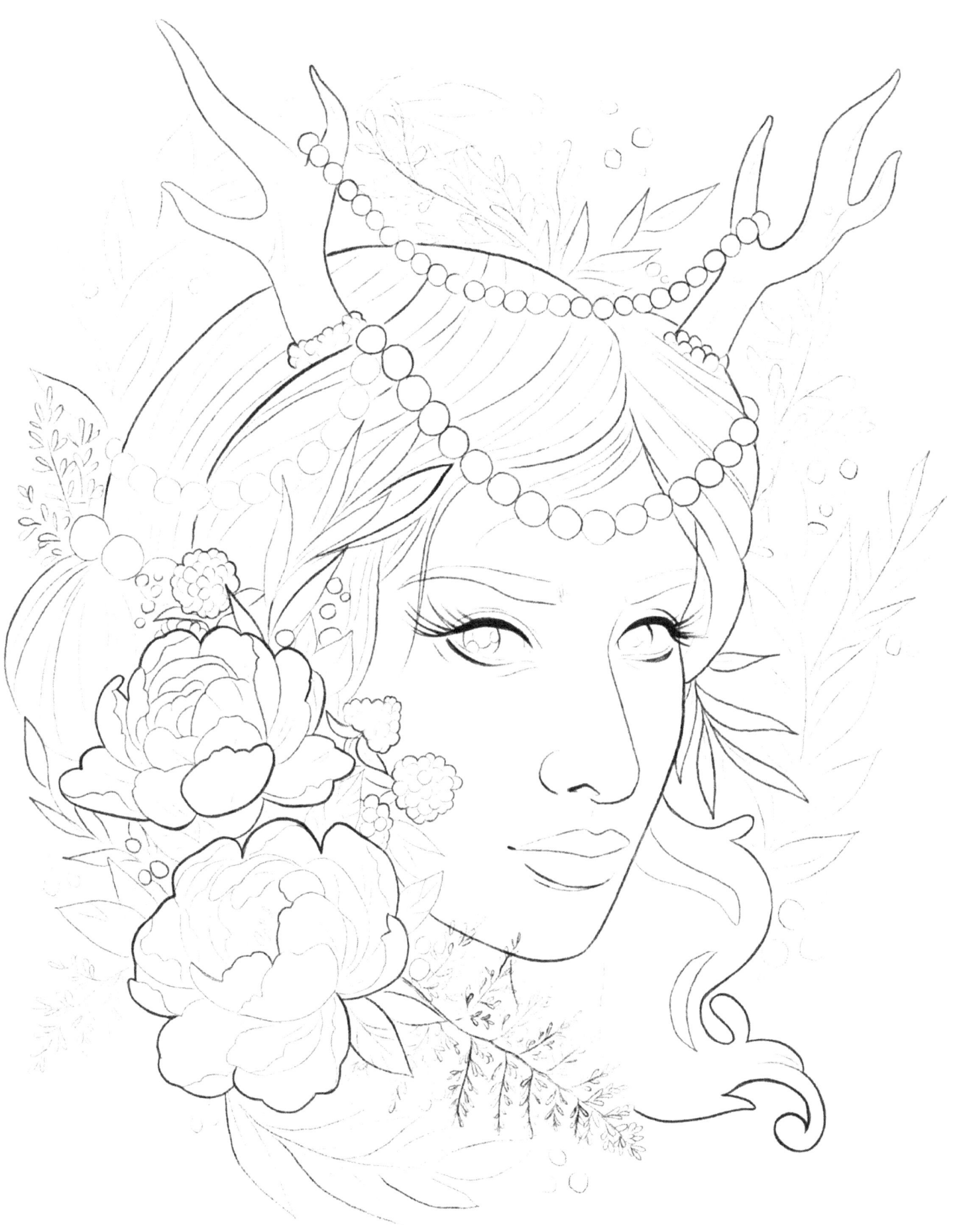

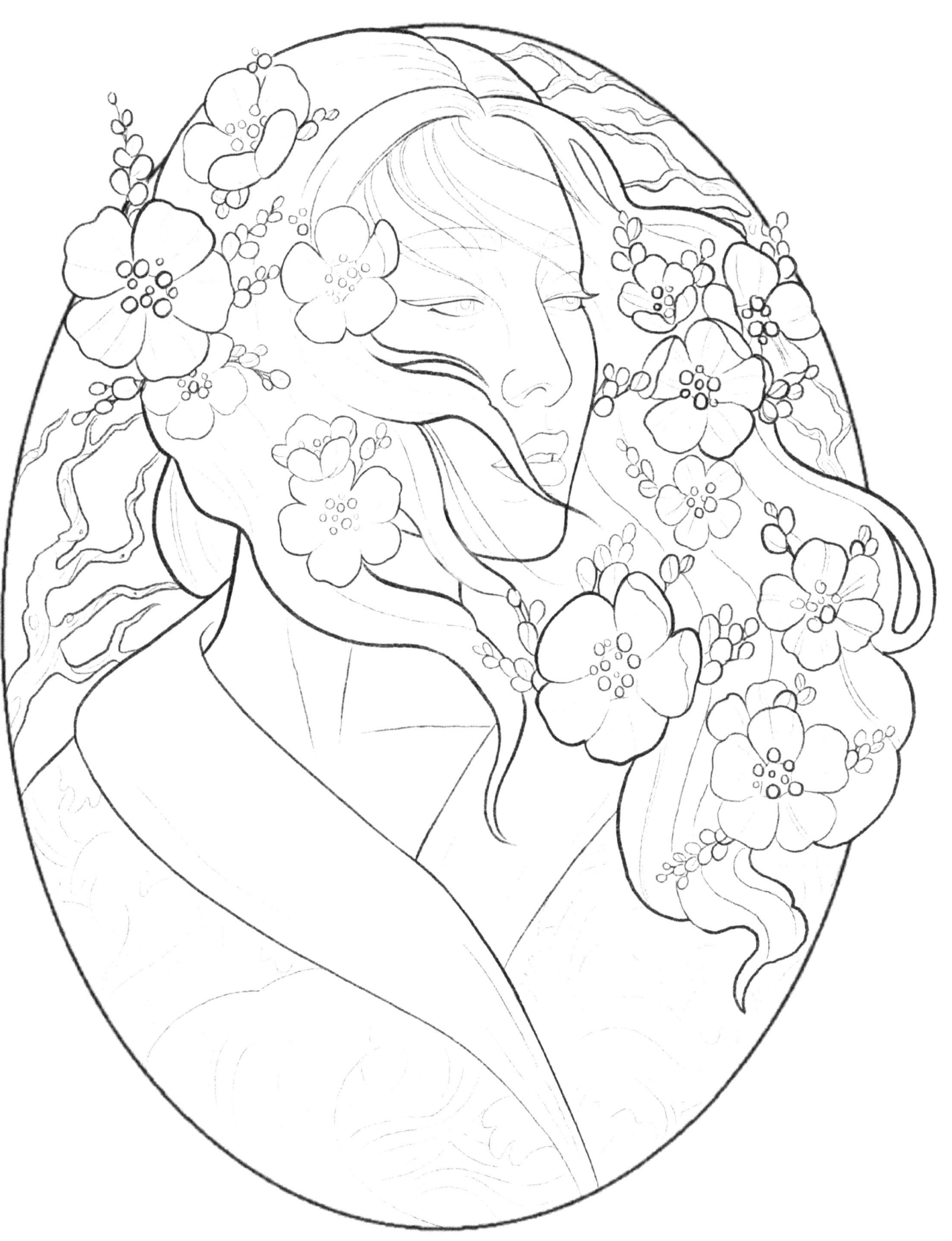

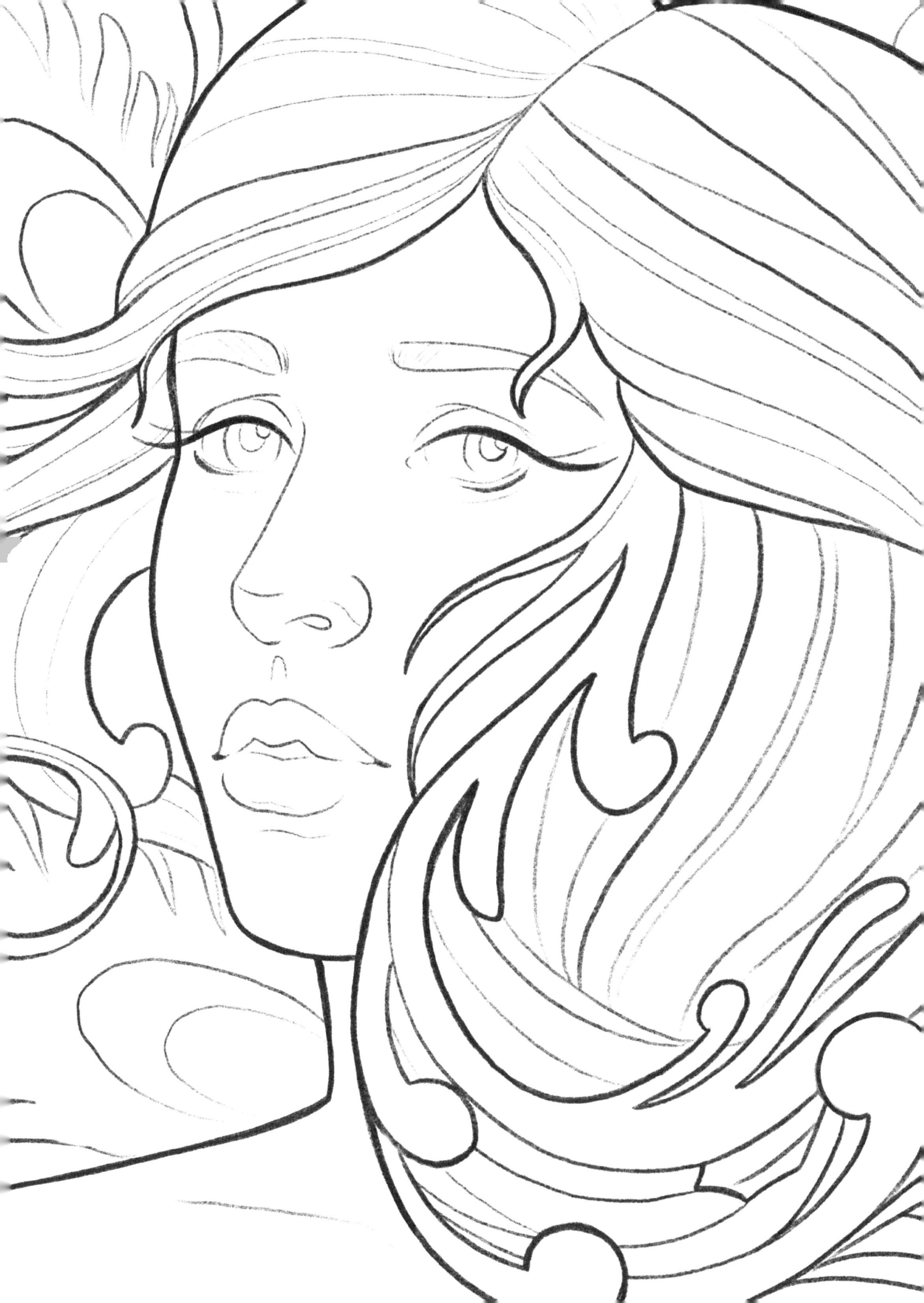

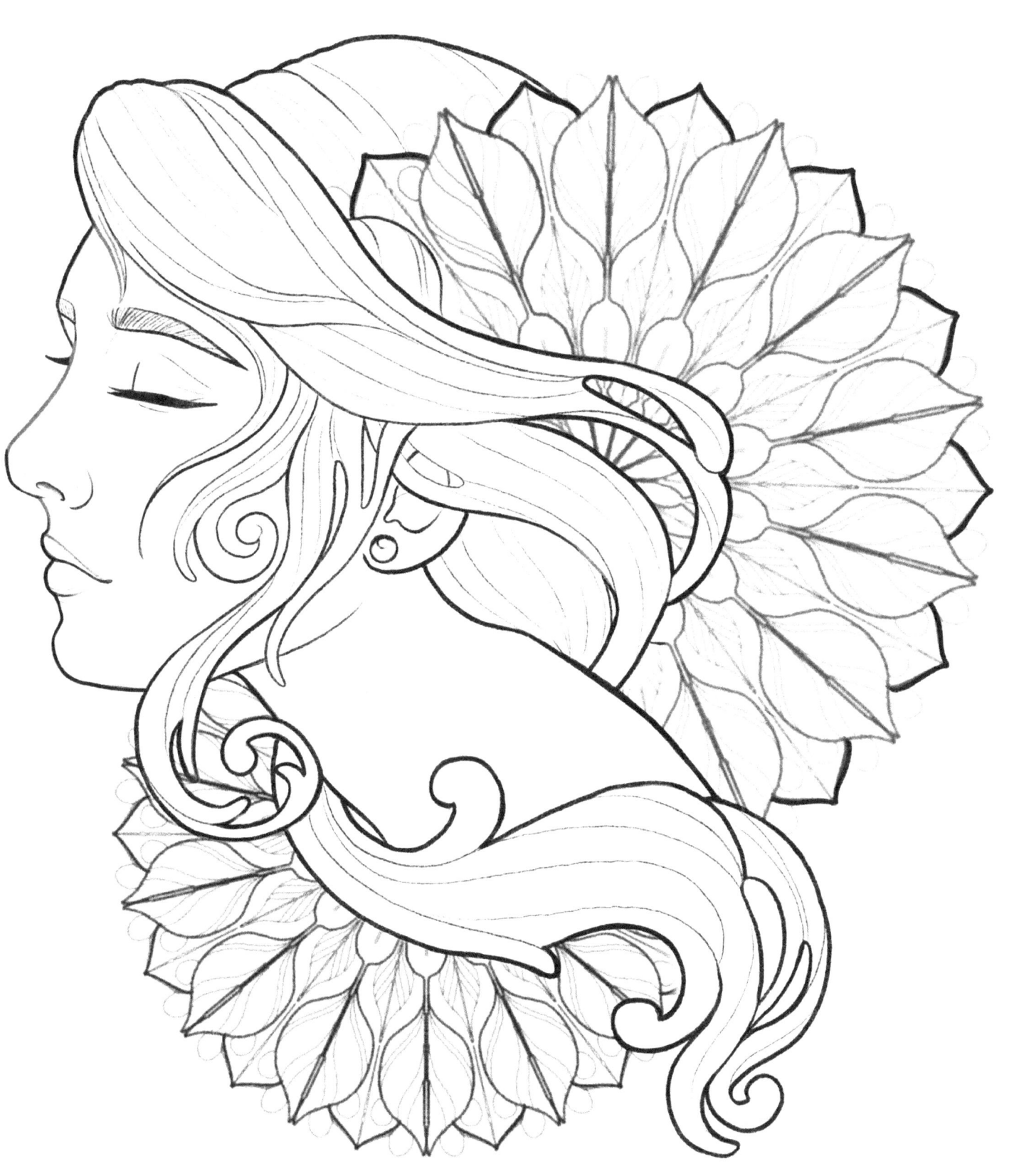

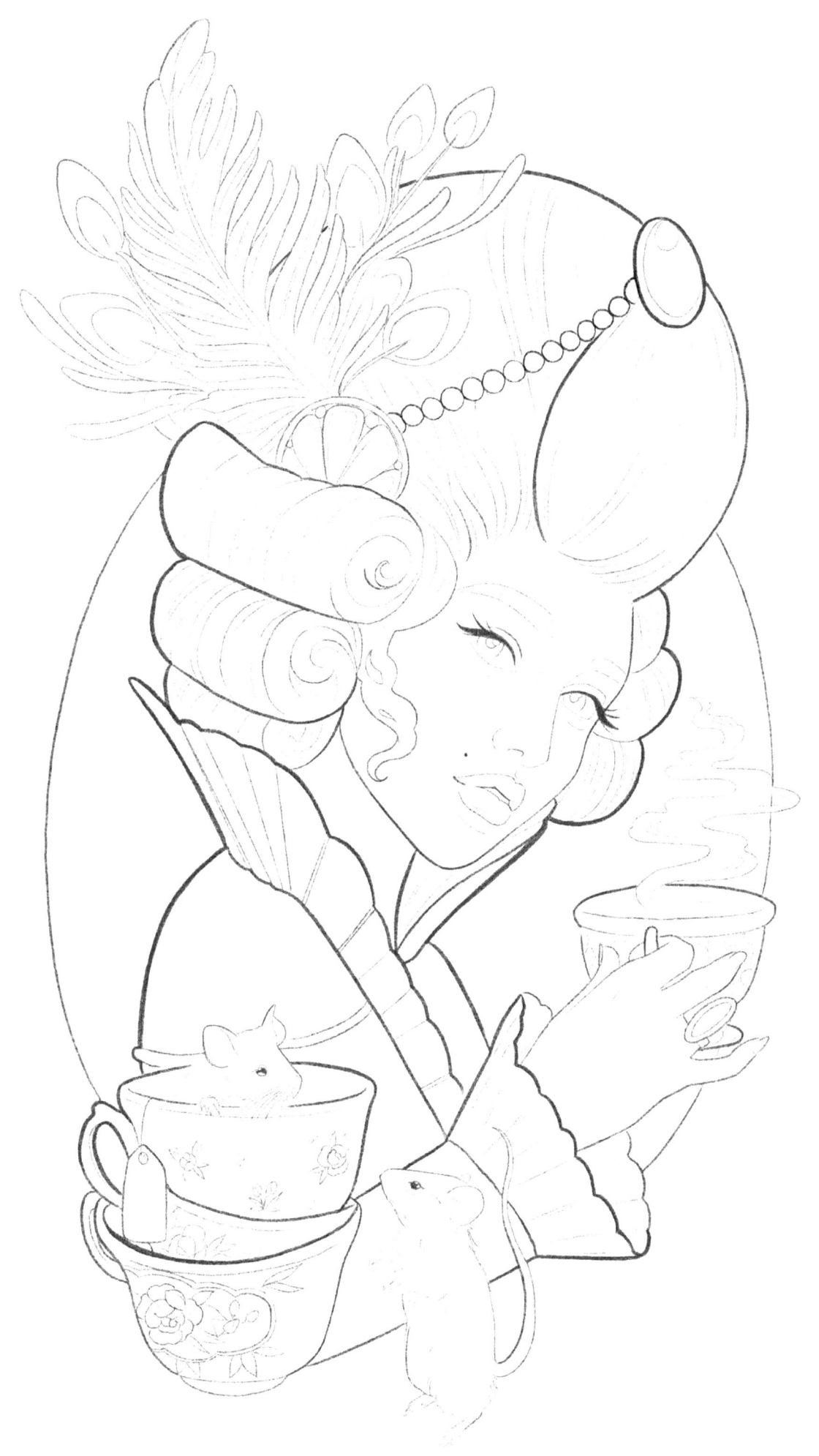

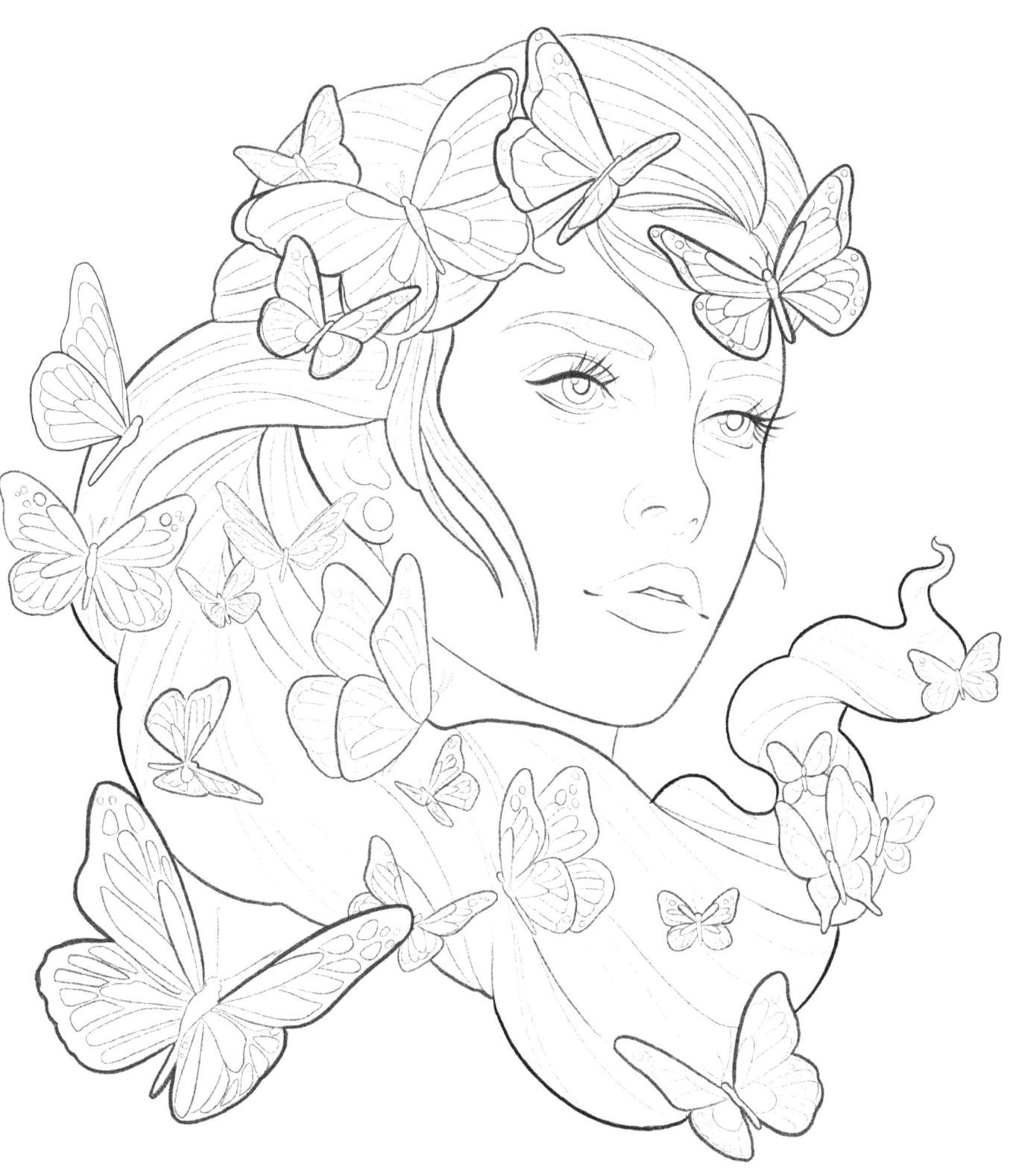

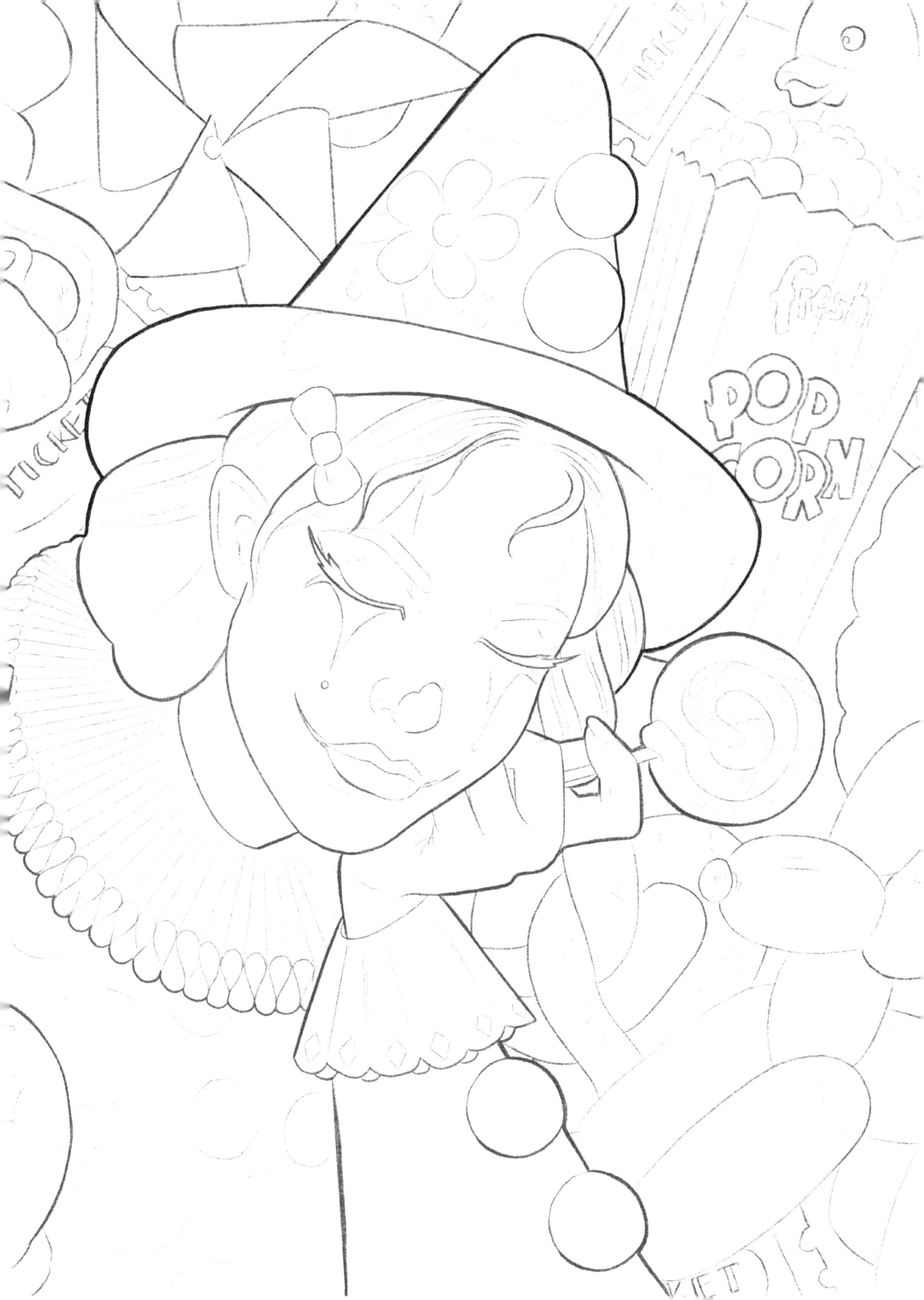

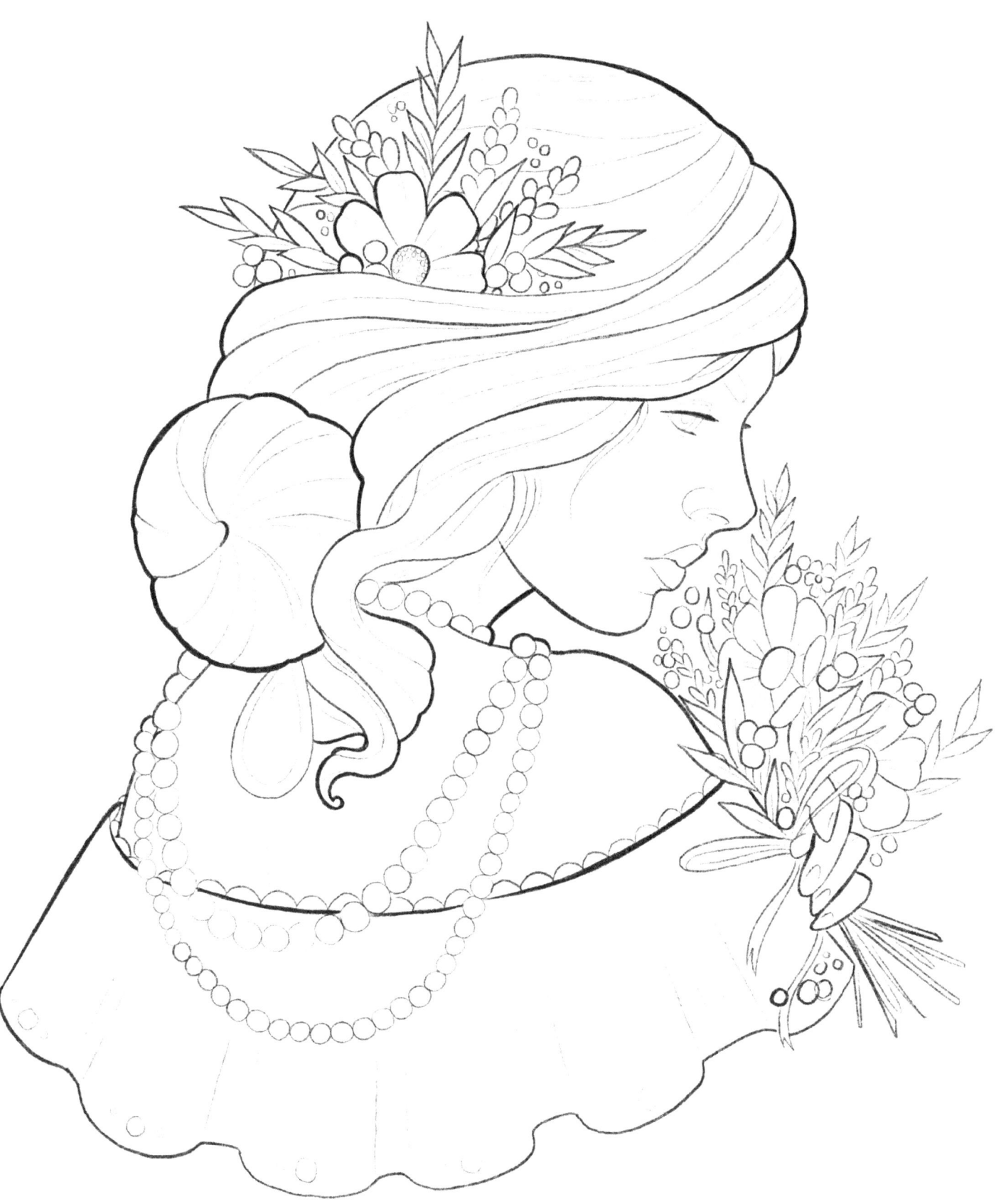

# ABOUT THE "AUTHOR"

MADISON TEASE IS A TATTOO ARTIST FROM
SALT LAKE CITY, UTAH WHERE SHE LIVES
WITH HER HUSBAND CHRISTOPHER
AND THREE FUR BABIES, MOLLY, WALTER, AND ANNIE.
MADISON GATHERS HER INSPIRATION
FROM ARTISTS LIKE ALPHONSE MUCHA, GUSTAV KLIMT,
AND EDGAR DEGAS; OBSESSED WITH TRYING TO CAPTURE
IMAGES OF BEAUTIFUL, STRONG WOMEN IN THE MOMENT.

THE IMAGES FOUND IN THIS BOOK ALL STARTED
AS CONCEPTS FOR TATTOOS, BUT NOW THEY ARE
HERE TO SHARE WITH YOU!
SHE HOPES THAT YOU WILL ENJOY
ADDING YOUR OWN MAGIC TO THESE DESIGNS!

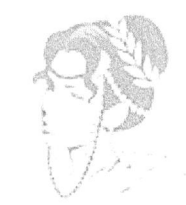

WE WOULD LOVE TO SEE WHAT LIFE YOU
BREATHE INTO THESE!

PLEASE TAG YOUR COMPLETED COLORINGS ON INSTAGRAM
@ MADISONTEASETATTOOS

www.ingramcontent.com/pod-product-compliance
Lightning Source LLC
Chambersburg PA
CBHW082253220526
45469CB00009B/2993